# Roads and Resources

Appropriate technology in road construction in developing countries

Edited by G.A. Edmonds and J.D.G.F. Howe

A study prepared for the International Labour Office within the framework of the World Employment Programme

An Intermediate Technology Publication

Copyright © International Labour Organisation 1980
Published by Intermediate Technology Publications Ltd,
9 King Street, London WC2E 8HN, U.K.
First published 1980
Reproduced from copy supplied
printed and bound in Great Britain
by Billing and Sons Limited
Guildford, London, Oxford, Worcester

ISBN 0 903031 69 8

---

The printing of this publication has been made possible by a grant from the Overseas Development Administration. The Intermediate Technology Development Group gratefully acknowledges their assistance.

The World Employment Programme (WEP) was launched by the International Labour Organisation in 1969, as the ILO's main contribution to the International Development Strategy for the Second United Nations Development Decade.

The means of action adopted by the WEP have included the following:
— short-term high-level advisory missions;
— longer-term national or regional employment teams; and
— a wide-ranging research programme.

Through these activities the ILO has been able to help national decision-makers to reshape their policies and plans with the aim of eradicating mass poverty and unemployment.

A landmark in the development of the WEP was the World Employment Conference of 1976, which proclaimed inter alia that "strategies and national development plans should include as a priority objective the promotion of employment and the satisfaction of the basic needs of each country's population". The Declaration of Principles and Programme of Action adopted by the Conference have become the cornerstone of WEP technical assistance and research activities during the closing years of the Second Development Decade.

This publication is the outcome of a WEP project.

---

The responsibility for opinions expressed in signed articles, studies and other contributions rests solely with their authors, and publication does not constitute an endorsement by the International Labour Office of the opinions expressed in them.

The designations employed and the presentation of material do not imply the expression of any opinion whatsoever on the part of the International Labour Office concerning the legal status of any country or territory or of its authorities, or concerning the delimitation of its frontiers.

# CONTENTS

| | | Page |
|---|---|---|
| FOREWORD | | 4 |
| INTRODUCTION | | 7 |

**Part I** **Institutions and Issues of Implementation**

Chapter 1 Appropriate road construction technology and the institutional framework. G.A. Edmonds and J.D.G.F. Howe — 13

Chapter 2 Road construction and resource use. G.A. Edmonds — 22

Chapter 3 Planning and administration of labour-based road construction programmes. B.E. Nilsson — 50

Chapter 4 Equipment for labour-based road construction. I. Barwell and J.D.G.F. Howe — 71

Chapter 5 The private construction sector and appropriate technology. A. Austen — 93

**Part II** **Case Studies**

Chapter 6 The "Roads and Labour" Programme, Mexico. G.A. Edmonds — 123

Chapter 7 The self-help approach, Afghanistan. G. Glaister — 135

Chapter 8 The Border Roads Organisation in India: labour-intensive construction on a large scale. Major-General J.S. Soin — 156

Chapter 9 Social and environmental factors: lessons from Iran. R.S. McCutcheon — 166

**Editors' Summary** — 192

## FOREWORD

In recent years, developing countries have been increasingly preoccupied with the need to create additional employment as a means of alleviating poverty. Attention has been paid to the feasibility of reducing unnecessary use of equipment in civil construction works with a view to making more effective use of labour. Although for many years civil construction works have been recognised as a means of employment generation, the notion that these works could be executed through the use of efficient labour-intensive methods is of a recent origin.

In this book, prepared within the framework of the ILO World Employment Programme (WEP), the editors, Drs. Edmonds and Howe, have selected a sample of operational programmes using labour-based methods (in India, Afghanistan, Iran, Mexico and Kenya) to throw light on the planning, management and administrative aspects of their widespread application.

Early WEP studies on road construction technology like the ones in Iran, Thailand and the Philippines were concerned mainly with question of the technical and economic feasibility of alternative techniques. Although some of these studies, in particular the one on Iran, did discuss the ways in which private contractors could be encouraged to use socially optimal methods through fiscal incentives and other governmental regulations, they were less preoccupied with the broader questions of organisation, management and large-scale implementation of labour-intensive techniques. It was first considered essential to overcome well-established prejudices on the parts of engineers and economists alike, against these techniques, by presenting hard facts based on field experiments. The case studies, especially the one in the Philippines, clearly demonstrated that the labour-intensive techniques need not be inferior, that certain construction tasks are economically viable whether one uses market or social price tags on physical quantities, that it is possible to devise technically efficient labour-intensive techniques.

The next objective of the technology research programme in this sector was to examine the constraints and opportunities in implementing these alternative techniques on a large-scale to alleviate the unemployment problem of the Third World. The papers and case studies in this book are in the series of these institutional investigations.

Conventional thinkers have criticised the use of labour-intensive techniques in construction on the grounds of their low productivity and slowness. For example, it has been argued that very low labour productivity makes these techniques inefficient. It is further maintained that labour-intensive methods tend to delay the completion of construction activities. Chief engineers who have fixed budgets and target dates for task completion are tempted to bring in bulldozers to do the job in time rather than having to rely on large number of labourers. It is generally forgotten that construction delays often occur not so much due to low labour productivity as to lack of adequate project planning, insufficient control over project schedules and poor designing. In principle, a given construction output can be produced by labour-intensive techniques with the same gestation lag provided the much larger work-force required is available or can be easily mobilised. Thus, given technical choice, length of construction may be considered a planning variable which can be manipulated by changing the degree of labour concentration. This indeed has been vindicated by the experience of the Government of Kenya with its Rural Access Roads Programme on which Chapter 3 of this book by Bertil Nilsson is largely based. Labour-based methods used under this programme did not necessarily lead to an increase in costs or duration of the projects largely because a special effort was made to reappraise and adapt conventional equipment-oriented systems and procedures (relating to bidding, procurement, training and administration) to the requirements of the labour-based programme.

Within the framework of WEP research on construction technology institutional studies are examining more and more the extent to which labour productivity could be raised through proper planning, better organisation and site management, improved tools and equipment and by incentive schemes including local participation of potential beneficiaries in road construction activities. Some of these issues are also discussed in various chapters of this book.

It is encouraging to note that despire the early prejudices of engineers and policy makers, accumulated knowledge of the viability of labour-based methods has led several developing countries, notably Kenya, Botswana and Ethiopia, to launch operational programmes experimenting in these methods with ILO assistance.

The WEP activities on civil construction technology are now being developed in a broader context of rural development. The types of roads to be built and the techniques to be used in building them cannot be divorced either from transport planning and infrastructure or from the choice of the type of vehicles to be used. Experience gained in road construction is also being applied to explore alternative techniques in small and large-scale irrigation works that can make significant contribution to the growth of agricultural output and employment.

Some of the chapters of this book were originally presented as papers at a Seminar on the Application of Appropriate Technology in Road Construction and Maintenance held in Manila in May 1977. This Seminar was organised by the ILO and financed jointly by the Swedish International Development Authority (SIDA) and the Asian Development Bank (ADB).

A.S. Bhalla,
Chief,
Technology and Employment
Branch,
International Labour Office.

**INTRODUCTION**

This book is concerned with appropriate construction technology in the building and maintenance of roads. It is one of a series resulting from the World Employment Programme of the ILO.

Traditionally, labour-based[1] methods have been viewed as a way of providing employment and/or income on a large scale; or as a means of mitigating the effects of disasters such as droughts, famine, earthquakes, etc. Their use has generally been conceived, planned and administered by, on the one hand, government planners and, on the other, relief organisations. Rarely has their use been initiated by those responsible for the execution of civil construction (i.e. engineers).

By drawing upon the detailed studies that have been carried out by the ILO and experience from recently executed labour-based programmes, the book shows that the use of more labour-intensive techniques can be technically and economically efficient. It also shows that the level of planning and organisation required for efficient labour-based programmes is no less demanding than that for equipment-based programmes. Moreover, as the existing systems in the construction sector of many developing countries are oriented towards the use of equipment, it often is necessary to pay careful attention to the detailed modification of these procedures so that labour-based techniques can achieve their full potential.

The book is in two parts. The first deals with the institutional framework within which the application of appropriate technology is proposed and with the various aspects of the implementation of appropriate technology. Having discussed the institutional framework it continues with a discussion of the major aspects of labour-based road construction, using as a basis the various ILO studies and programmes in Iran, Thailand, Nepal, the Philippines, India and Kenya. The following chapter, the author of which has been closely involved in the work of both the World Bank and the ILO, shows how the detailed planning and administration of a labour-intensive programme requires a different, though no less demanding, approach than an equipment-orientated programme. In particular, it indicates that the use of more labour-intensive methods has to be integrated into the procedures and systems of public works departments. This often requires that existing systems be modified as they are usually biased towards the use of equipment. The fourth chapter in this part discusses the potential for improving and adapting simple equipment to meet the needs of labour-based methods. If labour-based methods are to be adopted on a large scale, then the private sector will inevitably be involved. The final chapter in Part I describes the constraints on the growth of the domestic construction sector in Asia and shows how the application of appropriate technology could provide the means for the more rapid development of the sector.

Part II comprises four chapters describing on-going or recently completed labour-based programmes. However, because of the diverse conditions under which they have been formulated, there is a consequent variation in emphasis from one programme to the next. Thus, the Border Roads Organisation, India, was set up along military lines in a country which has traditionally used labour-based methods. The project in Iran, on the other hand, was much less ambitious and in a country with which one would not usually associate the use of labour-based methods. The Mexican programme is probably the largest of its kind and was initiated with little or no external assistance. The programme in Afghanistan is the odd one out in that it has been set up as a self-help programme and is more in line with the traditional use of labour-based methods as discussed above.

Finally, in the summary, the editors draw together the main aspects that arise from the preceding chapters and discuss the implications of the use of a more appropriate technology in road construction in developing countries.

**Notes and references**

[1] Because of the inefficiency of traditional methods used by labour, the term labour-intensive can no longer be considered adequate.

Whilst it was originally used to describe those techniques in which labour was used intensively, i.e. efficiently and effectively, there has been a tendency to apply the term to those techniques that are "labour-extensive", that is, where labour is used on a large scale but inefficiently for employment generation or other reasons, little attention being paid to improving productivity. To avoid confusion, the general term "labour-based" has been adopted. The terms "labour-intensive" and "labour-extensive" could then be used to differentiate between schemes which are concerned with the efficient use of labour and those in which employment creation or other societal objectives are paramount, respectively.

# PART 1 INSTITUTIONS AND ISSUES OF IMPLEMENTATION

## CHAPTER 1. APPROPRIATE ROAD CONSTRUCTION TECHNOLOGY AND THE INSTITUTIONAL FRAMEWORK

*by G.A. Edmonds and J.D.G.F. Howe*

The suggestion that the technology used in developing countries should be appropriate to the physical and financial resources seems at first sight so much of a truism that it hardly requires further investigation. Unfortunately, however, simple concepts often have very complex implications. In its most elementary form the suggestion is that in labour-surplus economies more labour-intensive methods would appear to be appropriate. However this elementary statement conceals a much deeper aspect of the concept of appropriate technology. Put bluntly, in accepting an economic policy based on technology which is appropriate to the available resources one is adopting a pattern of social and economic development.

In an age when social development has lagged behind the development of technology it is, perhaps, not surprising that the concept of appropriate technology has been seen as an alternative path by which developing countries can attain economic independence and stability. It is certainly true that the development strategies of the 1950s and 1960s which emphasised the rapid growth of GNP did very little to improve the living standards of the mass of the population. The expected "trickle-down" effect just did not materialise. In fact the real income of the rural population of many developing countries remained static or decreased[1]. According to the ILO the number of persons designated as seriously poor and destitute increased by 10 per cent or 120 million people between 1963 and 1972[2]. Of those considered seriously poor nearly 80 per cent live in the rural areas[3]. The near static condition of the income of the mass of the population of developing countries during the last 10-15 years is in sharp contrast to the rapid growth rate both in apparent per capita income and agricultural production. The indiscriminate use of modern industrial technology has been seen as one of the causes of the lack of distribution of the benefits of high growth rates[4]. Nevertheless it would be quite wrong to assume that by providing an alternative technological package one is dealing with the causes of poverty and unemployment. One must be absolutely clear that the concept of appropriate technology will have little effect if it is presented and implemented as a neutral package which will help to restore the balance of inequality within a given framework. Technology is not neutral nor is the choice of technology made in an economic or political framework which allows an equitable assessment of the available resources. The suggestion that "to intermediate levels of development there must correspond intermediate levels of technology"[5] assumes that the development process is neutral, free of political and social considerations.

There is little doubt that much of the technology being used in many developing countries is inappropriate in that it ignores the economic facts of life: that there is a shortage of capital and a surplus of available manpower. It is simple to show that if one applies the same level of investment per head that applies in the capital-intensive societies of the developed world to the developing countries, the level of employment created would be extremely small. (4.4 per cent in India, 5.1 per cent in Nigeria). But the acceptance of the concept of appropriate technology should also imply a political commitment to a strategy of development geared to the benefit of the mass of the population. If this commitment is not there then appropriate technology will be merely a useful gimmick for the traditional sectors of the economy. It will be viewed as a second-best alternative foisted on developing countries by well-meaning liberals from the developed world.

This book is about road construction. The preceding discussion may therefore seem a little out of place to engineers and planners concerned with achieving output targets within limited budgets. However the implementation of appropriate construction technology is not merely concerned with improving the productivity and efficiency of labour. It is also concerned with the institutional barriers to the application of a more appropriate technology. Whether these be due to education, to administrative standards and procedures set up in the past or to inappropriate design standards, they can be considered as part of the political structure in the broadest sense.

For example, if we look at the road network and administration of many developing countries we can see that they were a natural development when set in the historical context of the colonial period and the need to provide ready access for the export of the basic raw materials required by the industrialised countries. The focus of the transportation network was to the outside world; to ensure that exportable products were transported as quickly and efficiently as possible out of the country. The economies of many developing countries depended on the foreign exchange earned by the export of cash crops[6]. The need therefore was perceived as being for railways or high standard paved roads from the interior to the ports. The administration of road construction was generally centralised in the capital and either because of colonial tradition or because of the need to build up the primary network as fast as possible, the procedures adopted tended to be similar if not carbon copies of those used in the industrialised countries. Thus, the development of the road network was automatically locked into a developed country framework with the additional factor that it was geared to exportation rather than internal development. Little attention was given to the development of a transportation network which served the mass of the population who lived in the rural areas.

As far as technology was concerned, the techniques used were those that appeared to be most productive. The initiators of road construction programmes were often from the already industrialised countries. These countries had already passed from the use of labour-intensive methods to reliance on equipment for a variety of socio-economic reasons and they viewed the former as an inefficient means of production. However, in the industrialised countries, the historical development of construction technology reflects the resources of the economy at the time they were developed. That is, labour-intensive techniques were used when the availablility of investible funds was low in relation to labour supply whilst equipment-intensive techniques developed later when a greater level of investment was available in relation to labour supply. The memory of labour-intensive techniques is one of lower productivity. This, however, is principally related to the limited technical knowledge available at the time of the use of these techniques[7].

Thus, equipment-intensive techniques in the developing countries were introduced because in the industrialised country environment they were no longer viable. Little consideration was given to the fact that the economic conditions of most developing countries closely matched those of the industrialised countries at the time when labour-intensive techniques were considered appropriate.

Recently there has been a growing recognition that the potential for balanced growth in developing countries lies less in technological and economic dependence on the industrialised countries and more in providing stimulation for the development of the rural areas. This concentration on internal development has important implications since it implies a redistribution of the benefits of growth to the mass of the population. As far as road transportation is concerned this means an increasing emphasis on the rural road network. This will ensure not only that access is provided for social services, but that the potential for agricultural development and rural industrialisation can be achieved. It also implies a popular participation in decision-making and development. The emphasis should be on providing inputs into the rural areas which will stimulate growth rather than access to ensure the maximum level of exportation. If this type of development strategy, which emphasises the development of indigenous capacity and self-reliance, is pursued then appropriate technology can play a major role. The use of methods which rely on the efficient and productive use of labour can then be viewed in their true perspective as the most effective use of a country's natural resources.

The systems and procedures developed for road construction were, as we have seen, directly related to policies of export maximisation and rapid, centralised industrialisation. A change to a more balanced strategy of development which is also concerned with socio-economic factors will require that these institutional factors are reconsidered. Thus, the application of a more appropriate technology in road construction will require that the whole system of road planning, design, management and construction is reappraised.

Road construction consumes a large proportion of government investment[8]. If it were possible therefore to make the techniques used in road construction more labour-intensive, whilst being still efficient, then this large government expenditure could be used to promote employment and reduce the level of dependence on foreign imports and technology.

Apart from the obvious benefits, there are however other good reasons to consider road construction. There is, after all, a historical precedent for the use of labour-intensive methods. In 19th century Europe and America, before the advent of the internal combustion engine, roads were built by men using simple hand tools and animal-drawn equipment. Furthermore, in countries like India, roads built using large equipment are the exception rather than the rule. Then, again, the tasks involved in road construction are relatively simple and can be carried out by relatively unskilled labour who require little training. Much of the labour to be used will be from the rural areas and the tasks, tools and techniques utilised in the major activities such as earthworks are not dissimilar from those used in agricultural activities. In addition, the possible pay-off appears high. The amount of employment created per unit of investment is potentially large.

In most developing countries there is migration on a large scale from the rural to urban areas. Thus, whereas the average population growth rate is of the order of 2.5 per cent, in the cities it ranges from 7 to 10 per cent. Employment-creating activities which take place in the rural areas, as much of the road construction programmes do, could help to limit this migration.

Construction equipment is a major import in many developing countries. Furthermore, import of such equipment implies the future importation of spare parts. On the other hand, the cost of using the equipment is extremely high, requires skilled personnel and relies on fuel which is permanently subject to international economic factors. Any reduction in the level of equipment imports would reduce the pressure on limited foreign exchange resources.

In most developing countries the construction industry is dominated by large expatriate-owned companies. These companies, whilst fulfilling a vital role, tend to use the equipment-intensive methods and practices they are most familiar with.

The development of the local construction sector tends to be orientated towards the use of equipment-intensive methods. An acceptance of the viability of labour-based methods could allow local contractors to develop using indigenous methods and materials with which they are familiar.

The underlying rationale for the evaluation of labour-based techniques is that of the most efficient use of the available resources. Hand in hand with this evaluation would go an assessment of the most appropriate materials to be used.

There is also scope for the increased use of labour-based methods in the extremely important activities of road maintenance, particularly for routine activities such as ditch clearance, culvert maintenance and minor road surface repairs.

Finally, as we shall see later, there is a good reason to believe that the economic criteria generally used in project selection are biased against the use of labour-based methods.

The case for an evaluation, at least, of the feasibility using more labour-intensive methods is therefore very strong. It would be wrong, however, to assume that there are no objections to their use. Indeed some of the arguments against their use are quite potent and it is useful at this stage to present them.

First, and perhaps most important from the technical, economic and psychological standpoints, is the feeling that the use of labour-based methods will automatically produce a reduction in standards of construction. There is certainly some justification for this objection, particularly in relation to the compaction of earthworks and the final surfacing where it is true that it is extremely difficult to provide the same standard using labour-based methods. It would be wrong to suggest that these methods should be used when they produce inferior quality. Indeed, the approach should be that the methods used should be the most appropriate. If this means that equipment must be used, then that should be the solution. There is, however, another aspect to this issue. The standard of construction is specified by the design. Often the design is orientated towards the use of equipment and it is therefore not surprising that labour-based methods cannot meet the requirements. In addition, it can be argued, as we do later in this chapter, that the standards of construction may be artificially high and there exists an economic trade-off between construction standards and future maintenance costs.

Second, it is suggested that the productivity of labour-based methods is low. This naturally has repercussions in terms of the duration of projects. It is pointed out that low productivity either means an extension of the project time or that the number of labourers on the site has to be very high causing managerial and logistic problems. Unimproved, traditional labour-intensive methods do have a very low level of productivity. On the other hand, there is a large variation in the productivity of manual methods. In the activity of excavation for instance, the World Bank[9] noted a six-fold difference in productivities for different parts of the world. Clearly there is a potential for improvement of productivity given the right environment. There is therefore some validity in this criticism and consequently the improvement of productivity is a major factor in the development of viable labour-based methods. In one respect, however, low productivity may not be detrimental. There are certain construction activities which are non-critical, that is, the extension of their duration will not adversely affect the over-all construction time. On these activities it could be feasible to use labour-based methods even if they are not as productive as equipment.

Third, it is generally assumed that, partly because of low productivity and partly due to other factors, the cost of using these methods is prohibitive. There is, as we discuss later, an automatic bias in most project appraisal criteria against labour-based methods. Nevertheless some studies that have been done to try and make comparisons of labour- and equipment-intensive methods give credence to the idea. It is worth noting, however, that in general these studies attempted to evaluate what could happen if labour-based methods had been used on an actual project which had used equipment. The comparison is therefore carried out in a framework orientated towards the use of equipment. To equitably assess the most appropriate methods the whole construction process must be "opened up" to allow the consideration of alternatives. In the section on design in Chapter 2, for instance, we show that it is the total cost of construction that must be considered and that the design must be orientated towards the most appropriate techniques. In the final analysis, however, it is cost that is supremely important. The public works ministry or highways department has a limited budget for which it is accountable. It has to be sure that the best use is being made of that money. The use of labour-based methods must be shown to be not only socially but also economically appropriate.

Fourth, there is a strong feeling that the use of labour-based methods requires a high level of supervision which gives rise to high overhead costs not only on site but also in terms of additional training programmes. It is certainly true that these methods require a different kind of supervision. After all, one is considering the management of large bodies of men, not fleets of equipment. Whether the supervision is more costly is open to question, certainly experience so far does not substantiate this claim.

Finally, there are institutional forces within the construction industry which militate against the use of labour-based methods. The design methods, specifications, conditions of contract and methods of tendering all tend to reflect the dominating influence of expatriate consultants and contractors and their equipment-oriented framework. Even the methods of selecting contractors are often based on the amount of equipment they have and not on any ability to manage men. There is a natural inertia or resistance to change within the industry which could make the introduction of labour-intensive methods difficult.

In summary, there seem to be two categories of problem. First, the purely technical problems of low productivity, limitations of quality and high cost. There are then other problems which seem to have more to do with existing systems in the construction industry. These systems seem to be ill-suited to the introduction of labour-based methods. In the following chapters we look more closely into these aspects.

**Notes and references**

[1] ILO, *Poverty and Landlessness in Rural Asia*, Geneva, 1977.

[2] ILO, *Employment Growth and Basic Needs* Tripartite World Conference on Employment, Income Distribution and Social Progress and the International Division of Labour, Geneva, June 1976. Report of the Director-General and Declaration of Principles and

Programme of Action adopted by the Conference. Second edition, Geneva 1978.

[3] I. Ahmed, *Technological Change in Agriculture and Employment in Developing Countries*. Vol. 2. International Population Conference, Mexico, 1977, published by the International Union for the Scientific Study of Population.

[4] See for example F. Stewart, *Technology and Underdevelopment*, Macmillan, London, 1977.

[5] Intermediate Technology Development Group, information leaflet.

[6] This has even led to the substitution of cash for subsistence crops, to the extent that some developing countries are now net importers of subsistence crops in which they were previously self-sufficient.

[7] For a comprehensive coverage of historical/economic development of technology see F. Stewart, *Technology and Underdevelopment*, Macmillan, London, 1977.

[8] On average 60 per cent of total public investment in developing countries goes into construction and between 40 and 60 per cent of this construction investment is in road construction.

[9] *Study of the Substitution of Labour and Equipment in Civil Construction*. Phase I. International Bank for Reconstruction and Development, 1972.

## CHAPTER 2. ROAD CONSTRUCTION AND RESOURCE USE

*by G.A. Edmonds[1]*

### 1. Introduction

Since the early 1970s the ILO has conducted a series of studies and programmes which have analysed and evaluated the feasibility of using methods of road construction which rely heavily on the use of labour[1].

In this chapter the main conclusions of this work are presented and examined in the light of the experience of the ILO and also of other agencies and institutions, such as the World Bank, who have been concerned with this subject. The final section discusses the policy measures that could be adopted to assist in the implementation of appropriate technology in road construction.

### 2. Planning and administration

#### 2.1 *Choice of technology at the planning stage*

The use of appropriate technological construction methods requires that the whole construction process needs to be reassessed to ensure that at no stage is the choice of technology prejudged. Naturally, the further back one goes in the process, the less risk there is. Nevertheless, even at the overall planning stage there is some risk that, by default, the technology to be used is assumed. At this level, the consideration of alternative techniques would concentrate on such broad considerations as (i) what is the resource availability? (ii) are alternative techniques going to increase costs and/or duration? (iii) is it possible to integrate projects using labour-based and equipment-intensive methods?

In relation to the resources available, the supply of labour ready and willing to work would of course be of overriding importance in the consideration of using labour-based methods. The availability of labour, in sufficient numbers, is a prerequisite for any labour-based construction programme. Data must be collected, therefore, regarding this availability. The assumption that in labour surplus economies it is sufficient to establish the demand and there will be no difficulty as regards the availability of labour is not necessarily true. In this connection, it is also worth mentioning that the attitudes of the available labour towards work is an important factor which needs consideration. Earthwork is a predominant activity in most construction works. In certain countries earthwork activities rank below agricultural work in the hierarchy of employment. Therefore, it is necessary to ascertain the willingness of the available labour to accept employment on construction work.

The seasonal fluctuations in the demand for labour in agricultural activities are another aspect of labour supply and demand which have a significant effect on the progress of construction projects. It is of little value beginning a project using manual methods only to find an inadequate number of site workers during the harvesting season.

In making the assessment of labour that will be available for the construction projects, labour requirements for projects in various sectors running concurrently and also those required for the maintenance of existing infrastructure should be assessed carefully. It may be that, even if technically feasible, the labour supply situation precludes any chance of using labour-based methods. The ILO study in Pakistan was particularly concerned with this issue[2].

The integration of labour-intensive and capital-intensive methods is possible at the project level. It is of course also possible at the programme level. Let us assume that whilst it is as inexpensive to build a particular group of secondary roads labour-intensively it does, in fact, take longer. However, the secondary roads are of little value unless the main arterial to which they connect is constructed. There could be a case therefore for using the labour-based methods for the distributors and this could be recognised at the over-all planning stage. (In this simple example it is assumed that no other benefits are lost by extending the completion of the distributor roads.)

The choice of technology, therefore, can be assessed within a framework of an over-all planning time schedule. A careful analysis of this time schedule may preclude the use of a technology for reasons of delays in completion. On the other hand it might provide the opportunity for using alternative technologies because of the interdependency of one project on another.

## 2.2 *Centralised and decentralised systems*

The detailed planning of projects which depend to a great extent on the use of local resources is difficult to accomplish from a central administrative organisation. Nevertheless, it is also necessary for the planning and programming of projects to fit into the over-all framework of a national development plan. This can only be achieved effectively by a central organisation. In the case of centralised planning, although the central organisation may have control over the project proposal it is possible that it does not cater sufficiently for local needs. In the case of a decentralised system it is likely that the local needs will be identified; however, it may be difficult to integrate these proposals into a national plan. From the point of view of the most appropriate allocation of resources it is extremely important that, whether the emphasis is on centralised or decentralised planning, the final national road network plan is integrated and coherent. This will require that at this stage the over-all evaluation is made of the economic costs and benefits of making the maximum use of the resources available.

## 2.3 *Programme planning*

The use of labour-based methods may necessitate a large number of smaller projects or that large projects need to be divided into small units for efficient execution. This is true whether the work is to be undertaken by direct labour or by local contractors. Often the local contractors in developing countries are geared towards the use of indigenous resources and therefore tend to be more labour-intensive. The local contractors' resources are usually restricted and as a result where the projects are not divided into small works it becomes impossible for them even to qualify for bidding. In the use of direct labour on the other hand, various factors such as recruitment of labour, disbursement of wages, and procurement of material limit the size of projects that can be executed effectively.

2.4 *Programme administration*

The programme in Kenya,[3] in particular, has shown the importance of having effective administrative procedures for the implementation of programmes relying on the use of large labour forces. Often existing administrative procedures are orientated towards the use of equipment. In a labour-orientated programme it is vital that the procedures for pay, procurement of supplies, recruitment and reporting should encourage the smooth flow of operations.

Regular payment of workers is vital in achieving a high level of morale. Labour-based projects are often dispersed and require well-structured but decentralised systems of payment. In addition, although it is clear that piece-rate systems greatly improve productivity, many administrative procedures do not permit the use of any other than a daily-paid system of payment for direct labour.

The procurement of tools and equipment is of major importance in a labour-orientated programme. The administrative arrangements must provide for the even flow of these supplies to the project sites.

The evidence so far available suggests that it would be wrong to attempt to provide wholly new procedures of administration. What is required is the adaptation of the existing procedures to ensure that labour-based programmes are not put at a disadvantage.

## 3. **Project appraisal**

At some stage in choosing the most appropriate technology for a road construction project, it is necessary to make a cost comparison, for in the final analysis it is on the basis of cost, in its broadest sense, that decisions will be taken. It is extremely important therefore that the cost estimates accurately reflect the use of resources.

Of the data required for a reasonable evaluation, two problems are of particular importance in developing countries:

(i) unreliable statistical data, and (ii) use of inappropriate costing formulae, especially when hourly equipment costs are being estimated.

The first factor is fairly common and the obvious remedial measure is the development of a reliable data base. In the case of construction costs, reliable data are needed particularly for the estimation of hourly costs for various types of equipment. The project evaluator should beware of using the manufacturer's suggested unit costs, since conditions under which equipment is operated in developing countries are very much different from those in industrialised countries. The manufacturer's suggested unit costs tend, in general, to be lower than those prevalent in most developing countries. The main reason for this is that equipment yearly utilisation rates are usually much higher in industrialised countries than in developing countries. Methodologies for data collection have been described in an ILO manual[4].

The use of inappropriate formulae also seriously affects the reliability of estimated costs. In particular, many contractors and public works departments make use of inadequate formulae for the estimation of equipment depreciation costs. Often, these formulae tend to underestimate these costs, and therefore favour the adoption of capital-intensive technologies[5].

## 3.1 *The use of shadow pricing*

The evaluation of projects at market prices in developing countries often does not reflect the actual cost to society of utilising the resources available.

Road costs and benefits are usually estimated at "market" prices and/or institutional prices (i.e. prices fixed by government decree such as minimum wages, fuel prices, etc.). Furthermore, whenever costs and benefits are discounted to the present, an institutional interest rate is generally used for this purpose. Finally, whenever equipment and materials are imported, the local cost of these items is usually estimated on the basis of the official foreign exchange rate.

Evaluation of alternative technologies at market or institutional prices fails to allocate material resources in a way which maximises social welfare. In particular, the use of these criteria in the evaluation of alternative technologies in developing countries may lead to the unwarranted adoption of capital-intensive technologies, the wastage of scarce foreign exchange, and the increase of unemployment levels. There may therefore be a need to use adjusted market prices, often referred to as "shadow" or "accounting" prices, in order to offset the distortions inherent in market and institutional prices[6].

Shadow prices are a reflection of the opportunity foregone of using the resources in question for other purposes.

It should be stressed that the use of shadow prices in project evaluation is not just an economist's trick used to make labour-based technologies more attractive. The use of shadow prices does have a real and positive impact on the use of national resources. Nevertheless, the decision to adopt shadow prices rather than market prices in project evaluation is one to be taken by the highest authorities in the country, inasmuch as it is partly a political decision. The consequence of such a decision is that all public investment projects are evaluated on the basis of shadow prices.

The use of shadow prices in project evaluation is fairly straightforward once the adjustment coefficients are known. First, projects are evaluated on the basis of market prices, yielding estimates for various project inputs (e.g. skilled labour, unskilled labour, equipment depreciation costs, equipment operation costs, materials). Next, total costs should be disaggregated into skilled labour costs, unskilled labour costs, foreign exchange costs, local materials costs, etc. Finally, each of the above cost items should be multiplied by the appropriate adjustment coefficients provided by the planning, or other, government agency. The result is that all market costs will be translated into shadow costs. If an analysis based on shadow prices was applied to all proposed road projects, it is likely that a different hierarchy of priorities would emerge than if it had been done at market prices. Nevertheless, the total budget restrictions would be the same in either case. Shadow prices are therefore being used as a tool to distribute more equitably the funds available in relation to the relative scarcity of the resources.

ILO studies in Iran[7], Thailand[8] and the Philippines[9] clearly show that the use of shadow pricing eliminates the inbuilt bias in market analysis towards the use of capital-intensive methods.

27

## 4. **Design**

It is often said that labour-based methods are incapable of complying with accepted standards of design, the general implication being that these methods are therefore inferior. The standard of design referred to, however, is one that is appropriate in developed countries. It would be better if one questioned the appropriateness of using these design standards in a developing country.

### 4.1 *The choice of design*

One can approach the question of design and the choice of construction techniques in two distinct ways.

First, and most commonly, it can be assumed that the design is fixed and it is merely necessary to choose the most effective construction methods.

Second, the design, either in terms of the pavement or the geometric alignment, is variable to allow the consideration of alternative construction methods. This may or may not also imply that the maintenance and operating costs are fixed.

Let us consider the first case. The road is designed on the basis of certain economic and engineering criteria. In the simplest terms it goes from A to B and the route it takes will generally be governed by the economic objectives it hopes to achieve. The actual engineering standards of design will govern the type of pavement, the vertical and horizontal alignment and the structures required to carry the predicted traffic load. Let us look a little more closely at what this means in terms of the choice of technique. We will leave aside the question of the reliability or validity of traffic projections in developing countries, for this is a major issue in itself. The pavement design will generally be based on practice originating in the developed countries. There will almost inevitably be a bias towards equipment-intensive methods. This can happen in one of two ways. First, it is, of course, possible to produce the required strength and durability by using different materials. The laying of certain materials however does not lend itself to the use of labour-based methods. It is, for instance, difficult to lay bitumous material this way; however, an effective alternative such as, for example, stabilised soil can be laid effectively using labour. The first point therefore is that care must be taken not to specify materials which limit the scope of labour-based methods unless there is no alternative. Secondly, there is a natural tendency, reinforced by developed country practice, for the pavement thickness to be as small as possible. Put another way, the compaction of the sub-grade should be as high as possible. Whilst compaction achieves a variety of objectives, it is possible to consider that there is some sort of trade-off between sub-grade improvement and pavement thickness. Effective compaction being one of the operations that is difficult to execute using manual methods, a reduction in compaction (i.e. equipment) cost may be justified if it is not more than offset by the increased material cost of extra pavement thickness. In the recent ILO Manual,[10] an attempt has been made to quantify this trade-off. It should be recognised that in the case of a fixed design, there is no question of affecting the recurring maintenance and operating costs. The suggestion is merely that the design, being fixed in relation to certain standards, should allow the use of materials which may be more suited to the use of labour-based methods.

The question of the level of design standards leads us directly to the second case when the design is considered as variable depending upon the techniques involved. What we are really suggesting here is that instead of considering the construction costs only, we should evaluate the alternatives in terms of total costs. That is, we may be prepared to accept a lowering of design standards, reflected in a reduction in construction costs, if the increased cost of recurrent maintenance and vehicle operation did not exceed this reduction. Naturally one is thinking of modifying the design standards so as to make labour-based methods more attractive. For instance, it is often suggested that gradients should not exceed a certain value, say 6 per cent. This may require heavy earthworks when traversing hilly terrain. A relaxation of the gradient limitation may allow the road to take a more direct route, reducing the earthworks which will reduce costs and allow labour-based techniques to be considered. Naturally it would be necessary to assess whether the attendant increase in operating costs offsets the reduction in construction costs. Taking another example, the standards for minimum horizontal curvature are dictated by the design speed. A reduction in design speed would allow the road alignment to more easily follow the terrain contours, again reducing the level of earthworks and not only reducing cost but also favouring the consideration of labour-based techniques. In regard to design speed, it is in fact possible to quantify the relationship between design speed and construction costs for various types of terrain. Taken to its logical conclusion, the argument for choosing designs which minimise the total cost of construction, maintenance and operating costs could mean the actual change of route. If the direct route necessitated heavy earthworks, large structures and major rock excavation, it could be possible to use an alternative, more circuitous route, which minimises earthworks and structures, favouring the use of labour-based construction methods. This could of course produce a change in economic benefits which would have to be considered in the analysis.

The evaluation of total costs would compare the present value of the maintenance and operating costs over the life of the road with the construction costs for each design alternative. The evaluation should also consider the question of whether the maintenance methods to be employed will be capital-intensive or labour-intensive as there would clearly be additional secondary benefits with the use of the latter.

In a limited way an ILO study in Kenya[11] attempted this sort of analysis by assessing whether the total cost of providing a gravel road in the initial stage was less than that of providing an earth road with guaranteed periodic maintenance.

The detailed assessment of the total cost of design alternatives requires that much more attention is paid to maintenance activities. It is of little value justifying a particular design on the basis of a certain level of maintenance unless it is actually provided. Maintenance activities need to be financed, organised and implemented. The consideration of a certain level of maintenance in the economic evaluation is not a guarantee that this level will be achieved. Impassable or badly maintained roads throughout the world testify to the low priority that they are given.

### 4.2 *Structures*

The design of drainage structures, retaining walls and bridges is an integral part of the design of a road. In their design it is equally important to consider the most appropriate use of the resources available. It has been argued elsewhere[12] that for simple earth and gravel roads drainage is as important, if not more so, than the actual configuration of the road. A relaxation of gradient standards, for instance, may be possible if there is ample provision for the water to get away in the form of scour checks, drainage ditches and run-outs. Furthermore the provision of the right kind of drainage structures can prolong the life of the road whilst making use of indigenous materials.

Retaining walls are often constructed in concrete and as cement is generally an expensive import item, it is preferable to limit their size. If possible, one can eliminate them by the use of such alternatives as dry rubble walling. For revetments and abutments, the use of masonry is often a useful substitute for concrete.

A discussion of alternative bridge designs could be the subject of a separate paper. The main points to note here are that (i) the maximum use should be made of local materials; (ii) prefabrication is generally not an economic proposition; and (iii) there are often indigenous craftsmen skilled in building masonry or timber bridges of sufficient durability and strength. The first question to ask, however, with regard to bridge structures, is whether a structure is really necessary. For example, in many developing countries, a river that a bridge crosses is dry for 10 or even 11 months of the year. The economic consequences of closing the road for 4 to 6 weeks may not justify the expenditure on such a major structure. Another alternative is to consider the use of causeways.

## 4.3 *Appropriate education*

The whole question of design and the choice of the most appropriate construction methods is complicated by an education system in both developed and developing countries which tends to be orientated towards a type of construction industry that does not exist in the developing countries.

It is of course necessary to have a grasp of sophisticated, analytical techniques. They must be used, however, for designing roads which are suited to their environment. Designs which consistently require that a large proportion of the total construction cost goes in foreign exchange[13] when there are viable alternative techniques using local resources must be considered to be fundamentally inappropriate.

## 5. Road maintenance

In the section on design we stressed the importance of road maintenance. If it is carried out effectively it may be possible to limit the construction cost. If done badly it may mean that the estimated life of the road is drastically reduced.

It is, perhaps, because the cost of maintenance is a relatively small part of the total cost of road construction that little attention is paid to it. Indeed, it is often the case that in times of economic depression, road maintenance programmes are the first part of public works expenditure to be cut. However, this lack of emphasis is misguided and shortsighted. A well organised and well administered maintenance programme can defer the cost of major reconstruction thus releasing funds for other projects. Furthermore, whilst the foreign exchange costs of major reconstruction are considerable, of the order of 30 per cent, that of maintenance is generally less than 10 per cent. It is not therefore merely a question of deferment of costs but that the expenditure is channelled into local resources.

Maintenance comprises two elements. Routine maintenance, which is virtually independent of the amount of traffic. This involves clearing vegetation and keeping the drainage system clear. There is also the maintenance work that is dependent upon the traffic flow and is concerned with repairing damage caused by vehicles. Routine maintenance is relatively constant for all types of road varying only with the road width and the scope of the drainage system. Reparation maintenance is dependent upon the level of traffic and would increase with the increase of traffic. To provide an adequate level of maintenance, therefore, a basic minimum should be specified for feeder roads with little traffic and the level of maintenance should then be designated for each road in relation to its traffic volume. Unfortunately this rarely happens. Too often the maintenance budget is limited and only the major roads receive any maintenance at all.

It was suggested above that a greater investment in maintenance would have major benefits not only in deferring the reconstruction of the roads but also by conserving foreign exchange. Even in the developed countries, maintenance is a relatively labour-intensive operation. The operations are simple and can be efficiently carried out by manual methods.

Even regrading can be done by animal-drawn scrapers or graders. Unfortunately, many rural roads are built to a width greater than justified by the projected traffic flow to allow a mechanical grader to maintain them. This ignores the fact that there are labour-intensive methods available and also assumes that there will be a mechanical grader available to maintain the road.

For simple routine maintenance the scheme of having a "maintenance man" or group responsible for a section of road has been used in many parts of the world. Supervised effectively, and provided the worker (or group) is given the right incentives, this can be very effective. It has the advantage that the responsibility for maintenance is easily defined. This means not only that there can be effective supervision, but that the local people also know who is to blame if the road is improperly maintained. Often the worker or group can be given a certain minimum kit of tools (wheelbarrow, pick and shovel) to execute the work. Whilst there is an intuitive feeling that labour-based methods could and should be used in maintenance operations, it is clear that a more rational data base is required, so that the options can be quantified.

## 6. Project management

It is only in recent years that management principles have been actively applied in the construction industries of the developed countries. Apart from the social and public responsibility that a manager carries, it has become clear that the use of scientific management principles is vital for the effective implementation of projects. In principle the process of management consists of seven recognised processes which can be grouped under two main headings: planning and executive functions. In very broad terms the planning functions (forecasting, planning and organising), deal with material things whilst the executive functions (motivation, controlling and co-ordinating) deal with the human aspects of operations. The seventh process, communication, ties all the other functions together.

This introduction, whilst being commonplace to many, provides a useful basis for discussing the management appropriate to projects which employ methods which are orientated towards labour. One of the principal functions of management is to motivate the members of the organisation. In the industrialised countries this generally refers to projects utilising large fleets of equipment. If one replaces the major pieces of equipment by large bodies of men then it is clear that a certain amount of rethinking has to take place in relation to the various management functions defined above. In the following section we will look at what reorientation may be necessary in the light of the seven basic management functions.

## 6.1 *Forecasting*

By clearly defining the objectives of the project in terms of progress, duration and quality it is possible to specify in some detail the level of resources required at any particular time or location. This, of course, is a routine activity on any project. However, on a project involving the use of labour-based methods the forecasting function is given an additional role to play. It is first necessary to predict what will be the demand for labour. As in the demand for equipment, this will be based on the level of productivity expected. In recent years a sufficiently sound body of knowledge has been developed for estimates to be made for most labour-based construction activities. There are, in addition, various methods of making an assessment of productivity rates[14]. Apart from the reliability of data, the problems of forecasting labour demand are not severe. Labour supply is more complex. We have touched upon this problem in relation to programme planning. At the project level, however, it is necessary to assess the availability of labour for each activity in relation to the seasonal fluctuations of labour supply and the demand of other projects in the area. The project manager must have a clear idea of the relative levels of labour supply and demand so that the detailed plans can allow for any shortfall in supply and either defer activities until there is sufficient labour or use equipment for these activities. In its broader sense forecasting in the case of labour-based construction also means an assessment of the needs of the large labour force. The recreational, social, health and welfare facilities that must be provided need to be assessed at the initial planning stage. The number of supervisory personnel required will have repercussions in relation to any existing training programmes.

## 6.2 Planning

One of the major problems of using labour-based methods in road construction is that the flow of work has to be relatively even and not subject to large or frequent changes. A relatively stable labour force is more effective because morale is not reduced by constant hiring and firing and because management problems are reduced. Further, delays in projects that are equipment-intensive can often be easily dealt with by bringing extra machines on to the site. This is, often, simply not possible with labour-based methods owing to the number of workers that are required to do the same work as a machine. It is imperative therefore that (i) the project is planned in such a way that the labour demand does not vary enormously and (ii) that there is an even flow of resources to the project. As far as an even level of output is concerned, there are of course various techniques such as critical path network, PERT, bar or Gantt charts or the more recent Time and Location Chart, which can be used to arrange the activities in the optimum way. Once the basic requirement of a relatively steady labour demand is specified, these techniques are then used in the normal way. (Naturally allowances would have to be made for agricultural peak seasons.) These techniques can also be used to ensure the effective integration of labour-intensive and equipment-intensive techniques. For instance, it is often possible that those activities which are non-critical can be executed labour intensively and the planning techniques would indicate how this was possible.

The even flow of resources to a project is perhaps more difficult to achieve because the project manager is dependent upon external factors. Nevertheless, it will be possible to assess what resources are required at any time during the duration of the project. Of specific importance is the supply of hand tools, and any planning process should provide some indication, based on the life of each type of tool, of when deliveries will be required.

A planning system relies for its effectiveness on the reliability of the data used and the efficiency of the reporting systems which allow the system to be updated. A good planning system can provide the basis for effective control of the project. In the case of labour-based projects, which are particularly dependent upon an even flow of output, a system which will ensure a steady flow of resources is vital.

## 6.3 Organisation

Having predicted the requirements and planned their use the next step, prior to implementation, is to provide an organisation structure capable of executing the project. It can be argued that if labour-based methods are to be used the whole organisation structure used for equipment-intensive projects must be changed. Whilst there is some evidence from China that this can work, it is certainly not yet proven in general. Experience from the ILO studies has been that what is required is an adjustment of the structure to take account of the fact that the main resource being employed is labour not equipment. This means that gang size and distribution becomes extremely important. So also is the question of whether the gangs are arranged along functional lines or whether each gang or group of gangs is given a certain section of the road to deal with. Equally as important as the balance and distribution of gangs however is the type and level of supervision. How many workers can one gang leader effectively control? How many gang leaders can one foreman direct? Furthermore, there is the problem of ensuring good communication both down from the project manager and back up from the foreman and supervisors. The organisation structure can be extremely important when motivation and co-ordination is considered. In the former case the workers must feel that they are in touch with the project management and the objectives of the project. In the latter case good co-ordination is a function of communication which, in turn, is dependent upon an effective organisation.

## 6.4 Motivation

If a large labour force is to be used it is of paramount importance that they are motivated to achieve their potential in terms of output. It is fair to say that in most countries financial reward is the main motivation for good performance. The ILO studies have clearly indicated that workers paid on a piece-rate system produce much higher output than under a daily-paid system[15,16,17]. The system of pay, however, if it is to be a good motivator must not only be fair but must be seen to be fair. In the case of task or piece rates the targets set must be scrupulously defined to ensure that there is no exploitation of the worker.

Money however is not the only motivator. A sense of belonging, good relations with fellow workers and adequate social and welfare facilities are others. A good project manager will ensure that all these aspects are well taken care of.

### 6.5 *Controlling*

In the discussion on planning we noted that a good system will ease the problems of control. The physical and financial control of projects can be relatively simple as long as the original plan is constantly updated by means of data derived through an effective communication system. The supervisory staff must therefore be trained to provide clear and concise information regarding attendance, output and future requirements. An effective communication system must exist which allows this information to be channelled to the project management for evaluation, decision and action. Not only will this ensure that the project is provided with the resources required at the right time but also it will pinpoint inefficient working or work that is behind schedule. This can be immediately investigated. In this way a good control system can instil in the workers a feeling of participation.

### 6.6 *Co-ordination*

If labour-based methods are to be used it is likely that the number of supervisory staff will increase. The methods may also be integrated with the use of equipment. To ensure that integration is possible and that the large labour force is working as a coherent mass, not as a set of independent units, it will be necessary to bring the supervisory staff together at regular intervals to discuss the work programme. This would also be the time when labour relations problems could be discussed.

Finally, we can provide no better summary of the problems involved than the words of a famous writer on construction management[18]. "Not only is it necessary for a manager to be able to organise technologies but he must also be capable of organising individuals. He must be able to view the management activity as a whole and not from the bias of his own particular education and training. In the organisation of human beings it is necessary for the manager to realise that improvements in the workers' physical and social conditions together with the sharing of a sense of participation in the enterprise are the two effective prime movers of effective performance."

## 7. **Tools, equipment and techniques**

Most textbooks on construction management will almost certainly have a section on the choice and utilisation of construction equipment. A typical phrase from a well-known book[19] reads "correctly chosen and well operated plant will enable a construction project to be completed quickly and economically". Given that on a road construction project in the developed countries, equipment may account for upwards of 50 per cent of the total cost, it is not surprising that so much attention is paid to this item. If the resource utilisation is changed, however, and it is labour which is the predominant cost item then it is clear that much more attention has to be paid to their organisation and level of productivity. The labourer does not, however, work with his bare hands, he uses tools and simple equipment. In projects which are labour-intensive, therefore, the choice of the right sort of tool is as important as the choice of the right type of machinery in a capital-intensive project[20]. The cost of tools is not normally a major item even on labour-based projects, being generally of the order of 5-10 per cent of the total. It is their effect on the productivity of labour, however, which is of particular importance. Few detailed studies have yet been done on the difference in productivity for workers with "good" and "bad" tools[21]. Nevertheless all the experience reinforces the intuitive feeling that a well-designed, well-manfactured tool that is appropriate for the task increases the level of productivity.

### 7.1 *Appropriate tools*

If we are to invest money in the use of labour-based methods it will be necessary to spend much more time in considering the most appropriate tools for the particular job in hand[22]. A labourer is perfectly well aware of the most effective method of using traditional tools; what is needed is the most effective shape or type of blade so that, in the case of a hoe, for instance, it cuts each particular type of soil in the most effective manner.

In the consideration of appropriate tools, the first lesson to learn is that we must beware of imposing preconceived notions of what is the best tool for a particular job. Many of the basic activities of road construction and maintenance, such as excavation, loading and spreading, have counterparts in agricultural work. The labourers employed for road construction will generally be quite familiar with the most appropriate tools. Simple expedients such as reinforcing the blade of the tool at critical points to make it more durable for heavy excavation work seem to be the type of improvement that can be made. On the other hand, construction activities are much more demanding than agricultural ones and the tools used may have to be correspondingly more robust.

It is when the activities of workers become interdependent, such as in excavating and loading, or where the operations are markedly different from agricultural activities such as compaction, bitumen spreading or hauling with light equipment, that there is scope for the implanting of new techniques or the modification of existing ones. Consider for instance the question of haulage vehicles. Such methods as wheelbarrows, small trucks on rails, headbaskets, and animal-drawn carts are all generally in use in agricultural work. However, workers are used to using them individually and their design can often be improved in relation to the haulage of soil or aggregates. The wheelbarrow, for example, apart from being generally poorly manufactured is often also badly designed. The weight distribution is wrong, the size and type of wheel is ill-suited to construction sites. Furthermore the efficient use of wheelbarrows often requires a careful consideration of the balance between the loaders and the haulers.

Animal-drawn carts are often used in rural areas for the transportation of produce. The unloading is carried out by hand so as not to spoil the saleable goods. As far as the movement of soil in construction works is concerned, one of the main objectives is to unload the cart as fast as possible. Some system of tipping or bottom discharging would therefore have obvious benefits.

For long-haul distances it may be appropriate to use trucks or tractors and trailers. The important point to mention here is that the integration of labour-intensive and equipment-intensive methods requires special care. It is of little value asking labourers to excavate and load in a similar fashion to machines. If they are asked to load into trucks or trailers the height of loading must be appropriate and furthermore the size of the truck must not be so big that it requires such a large number of workers to load it that they are in each other's way.

The work carried out so far indicates that even for those road construction and maintenance operations which are not directly comparable to agricultural activities it is possible to adapt and modify agricultural equipment to do these operations effectively.

## 7.2 *The scope for intermediate technologies*

In recent years a great deal of attention has been given to the idea of developing so-called "intermediate" techniques. These would be oriented towards the use of labour whilst reducing the level of physical work by the use of small-scale mechanical devices. The idea that these intermediate techniques provide a missing link between labour-intensive and capital-intensive technology has gained some credence. In the studies on road construction, at least, this idea has not been well substantiated in practice[23]. The evidence suggests that there is scope for major increases in productivity by the selection of appropriate tools and the modification and adaptation of traditional techniques. It has not been shown that it is possible to implant alternative technologies to any noticeable degree. This, of course, may purely reflect the fact that for most construction and maintenance activities there are obvious traditional alternatives which can be made effective.

## 7.3 *Techniques and work balance*

The specific problems of site organisation and planning have been discussed in section 5. It is worth mentioning here, however, that the productivity of particular tools and equipment often depends on the organisation of work. The disposition of labourers excavating, loading and hauling can make an enormous difference in the over-all output. Two simple examples will illustrate the point. In the operation of excavating, loading and hauling material using labourers and tractors and trailers, the most expensive element is the tractor. It must therefore be working full time for over-all economic efficiency.

This can only be done if there is the correct balance between the number of labourers, trailers and tractors.

In the operation of surfacing using tar spray and chippings, it is imperative that the rate of spreading of chippings is synchronised with the rate of tar spraying. Further, the roller that is used must also have an output that is in keeping with the rate of surface production. If labour-based methods are used for spreading and spraying the gang balance must be correct for output to be matched.

## 7.4 *Procurement systems*

The provision of hand tools and light equipment for a project using equipment is of relatively minor importance. In a labour-based programme it is absolutely vital that the requisite number of small tools are provided in the right place at the right time, otherwise the work will stop. It will often be necessary to develop special procurement systems for labour-based programmes and to provide detailed specifications to manufacturers. Certainly the system of least cost tendency without specifications should be avoided. Furthermore, the increased attention that has to be paid to well designed and well maintained tools will place a much greater emphasis on having well qualified personnel to direct the provision and procurement of tools.

## 7.5 *Small-scale industry development*

This aspect is far too broad a topic to deal with comprehensively here. Nevertheless the implementation of large-scale labour-based construction programmes could have important repercussions on the development of small-scale industry. Certainly if there were a capability in the rural areas to manufacture the tools and light equipment required this could be a major area for effective development investment. There are of course many problems such as quality control, transportation costs, co-ordination, centralised tendering systems, etc. Nevertheless, small-scale industry development is one of the potential secondary benefits of labour-based construction programmes.

In Kenya, the World Bank has already carried out work to assess the scope for the local manufacture of the tools and equipment required for the Rural Access Roads Programme.

The initial findings of this study suggest that the problems are more to do with the basic inflexibility of administrative systems rather than any inherent lack of capacity in the manufacturing sector.

## 8. Policies for larger-scale implementation

In the previous pages the detailed problems of using more labour-based methods in road construction have been discussed. In the long term the concern is with the most appropriate use of resources in the construction of roads in the developing countries. The use of appropriate technology is not an emergency measure to counteract unemployment. It will do this but it is much more basic than that. The use of the most appropriate technological methods will automatically reduce unemployment because it will be using the available resources, including labour, in the most appropriate manner. It is, therefore, not merely a question of providing a proper framework of design, planning and management. The long-term, large-scale implementation of more appropriate technological methods in road construction, as in other sectors, will require that various policy measures are adopted in keeping with the shift away from the technologies which are patently inappropriate but for various reasons are presently preferred. In this section an attempt is made to present various measures that could be adopted. Where possible, examples are given of attempts that have been made to implement these measures.

### 8.1 *Fiscal policies*

In section 3 the use of social cost benefit analysis was discussed. This is a tool which can be used to take account of the distortion of market prices in developing countries. We saw that this distortion tends to favour capital-intensive methods. The use of accounting or shadow prices does not make any change to the actual prices, it merely takes account of the distortion to give a more rational allocation of resources. In the public sector the assessment of the most socially profitable techniques can be made on the basis of the shadow price coefficients provided by a central planning agency. The manager in the public sector then executes projects up to the maximum number his market budget will allow based on the accounting prices. In the private sector, however, the use of social accounting would be extremely difficult to implement. It would definitely require some form of government intervention to ensure that the contractor perceives that there is no loss in profit if he uses the alternative technologies. In the long term, however, the use of these technologies should prove to be profitable and a great deal depends upon educating the private sector in the use of labour-based methods. The government can, however, take various financial and fiscal measures which would assist in the acceptance and implementation of appropriate technology in road construction. These range from the very simple to the very complex. They are discussed below.

(a) *Surcharge* — one very simple method for allowing for the distortion of prices is to accept that it exists, to recognise that it favours equipment-intensive methods and to take the labour-based alternative where it is technically competitive as long as the market price is not more than a certain percentage more expensive than the capital-intensive methods. In the Philippines this has been done and labour-based methods are accepted if the increase in cost is not more than 10 per cent. In a way, this is an implicit social accounting procedure as it implies that the distortion in market prices is of the order of 10 per cent. This may seem crude and would, of course, require substantiation. However, given the complexity of the calculations to provide social prices it may be the most acceptable.

(b) *Tariffs on imported equipment* — in an effort to promote import substitution and to protect domestic consumer goods industries, many developing countries have adopted systems which provide high tariffs for consumer goods and low tariff rates for capital goods and raw materials. As far as road construction and maintenance is concerned this has the effect of allowing the importation of construction equipment at low tariff rates and thus effectively distorting the real cost to the economy of using the equipment. There are various ways in which this problem can be solved. One is to provide discriminatory tariffs on equipment which would be used on activities that can be carried out labour-intensively. This may, of course, be extremely difficult to implement in practice as a machine may carry out various functions some of which could not be done labour-intensively. An alternative is to make the importation of equipment dependent upon the provision of a licence which would be provided by the government only after it was convinced that the equipment was needed.

(c) *Adjustment of the market rate of interest* — many governments impose low ceilings on interest rates in order to prevent private banks from exploiting their monopoly power. However, if the capital market does not function properly low ceilings may have negative effects. Small investors in the unorganised sector are often unable to borrow money since the banking institution prefers to deal with the modern organised sector, where risks of default seem to be lower. Under these conditions, large contractors can easily borrow money to import construction equipment, and find it profitable to do so since the low ceilings on interest rates result in a decrease in the equipment rental rate. In some cases, moreover, given high inflation rates, low ceilings on interest rates imply a negative real interest rate on loans, and imports of equipment and the adoption of capital-intensive technologies becomes even more attractive. The proper government policy if there are low ceilings on interest rates is to remove the ceilings completely or to set them at much higher levels. High ceilings on interest rates will lead contractors to think twice before asking for loans in order to import construction equipment, and may thus induce them to reconsider their position with respect to efficient labour-based technologies[24].

(d) *Taxation of owned capital equipment* — a number of factors including low ceilings on interest rates, difficulty of importing spare parts for construction equipment, lack of proper equipment for repair and maintenance facilities — tend to make contractors import more pieces of equipment than may be strictly necessary in order to be sure that construction work will not be slowed as a result of lack of equipment. The government may put an end to this situation by imposing a tax on owned capital equipment. The cost of keeping construction equipment idle will therefore increase, and contractors will refrain from importing more equipment than is really needed. Furthermore, the imposition of such a tax will increase equipment rental rates. A tax on capital equipment is, however, difficult to administer. The government must annually assess the value of pieces of equipment at various degrees of depreciation. Needless to say, such an assessment is difficult to make and may lead to a large amount of litigation between contractors and the government. This type of government intervention is therefore not very practical and should not be attempted unless other types of action are not politically or economically feasible.

(e) *Wage policies* — the question of the most appropriate measures in relation to wages is perhaps the most difficult of all. This is partly because the difference between the market and shadow wage is often so marked. Other issues such as minimum wage legislation and trade union activity also have an effect.

Action in relation to wages is often seen as an effective way of favouring labour-based methods. All too often, however, the action is counter-productive because it directly interferes with market supply and demand. For example, the use of wage subsidies has been advocated. In its simplest terms this is the payment, by the government, to the contractor of a subsidy for each man-day of unskilled labour used on a project. Unfortunately, the result of this is that the contractor can continue to use capital-intensive methods, the increased labour force stands and watches[25] and the contractor pockets the subsidy. It is not sufficient to make it financially feasible for contractors to use methods which require more labour. They must also be convinced of the technical and managerial efficiency of these methods.

Finally, in regard to fiscal policies a comment from the Iran study[26] is particularly apt. "The argument concerning the relative merits of specific tariffs, quantity restrictions and wage subsidies does not turn on any simple notion of economies in government finance. The issue is basically one of ease of administration and relative efficiency of the set of measures adopted. Tariffs or quantity restrictions would appear to have a certain appeal as they are more easily administered than a direct wage subsidy. By themselves, however, they will not guarantee the adoption of appropriate technology. In the final analysis it will be the practitioners who choose the technology and any fiscal measures must go hand in hand with the appreciation of the technical feasibility of using appropriate technological methods."

## 8.2 Policies on standards and specifications

The ILO's employment strategy mission to Sri Lanka noted that "the problems in the construction industry were aggravated by the stolid enforcement of regulations, professional codes of practice or contractual procedures, the inadequacies of which have long been recognised in the very industrialised countries from which they were copied; copied moreover in the face of unquestionable evidence of their ineffectiveness in local conditions."[27] The situation in Sri Lanka is probably no different from that in many other developing countries. The unsuitability of European standards and specifications is most blatantly illustrated by such examples as the application of snow-loading criteria for roof construction in tropical Africa. Less obvious, but more common, however, is the specification of materials, methods of working and testing procedures which would be perfectly appropriate in Europe and North America but not in the developing countries.

There is no suggestion here that the systems and procedures used in the construction industries of developed countries are inefficient. Within their own environment they are generally effective. To expect them to work as efficiently in an environment where the basic economic situation is totally different, where the administrative systems are limited and where the information flow to the local construction sector is poor is somewhat optimistic. The basic dichotomy in construction caused by the division of responsibilities for design and construction becomes an even greater problem in countries where contractors are struggling with the basic problems of lack of financial and managerial expertise.

In regard to specifications and codes of practice therefore, governments need do no more than make an investigation of whether they are orientated towards the environment in which they are supposed to operate.

As regards methods of tendering it is clear that certain aspects of the normal tendering procedures are biased towards the use of equipment. One can think of the selected tender where only those with, among other things, a minimum plant holding will be eligible to tender. As far as government is concerned what is recommended is a more flexible approach to tendering procedures. These procedures were developed in the industrialised countries where there is an inherent tradition of contract responsibility and where the design, construction methods and procurement of materials are already institutionalised. They may apply also to vast development projects: however it would be surprising if they are wholly appropriate to construction industries whose members have relatively limited financial and managerial resources.

## 8.3 The influence of foreign consultants and contractors

If one accepts that infrastructure development is vital to economic development, it almost goes without saying that this implies some form of foreign involvement in the construction industry. This may merely be in the form of feasibility studies or managerial assistance. More commonly it will involve the use of foreign consultants and contractors. Properly arranged, their involvement can be mutually profitable. Unfortunately certain conflicts often present themselves. It has already been noted that procedures and systems with which large foreign firms are familiar may not be appropriate. Of more direct importance is the fact that, as the ILO's study in Iran showed[28], foreign firms will draw their technology from an international market in which innovation has consistently moved in the direction of equipment-intensive methods. As the consulting engineer is often involved at the feasibility, design and supervision stages, the technology used is dictated by his expertise and background and only too rarely by a detailed consideration of the most appropriate resource allocation. In addition one has a contractual system based on the industrial country practice, and a contractor who, if not foreign or foreign-owned will have been schooled in the efficient use of equipment; it is not surprising therefore that the technology chosen is extremely capital intensive.

The use of foreign expertise in the development of a country's infrastructure is a fact of life and has many beneficial effects. Properly handled, foreign firms can be a great asset in assisting in the growth of the local construction sector. It would be wrong however to view the activities of foreign firms in any philosophical way. Principally, their object is to make a profit. Whilst governments should support this objective it should also ensure that profit is generated in a beneficial way for the country. This means that when the government, as a client, hires a consultant to carry out a feasibility study for a road project, it makes it quite clear that the study should assess the construction technology to be used. It means that in its dealing with foreign contractors it should insist that labour is used to the fullest extent compatible with technical and economic efficiency whilst the importation of equipment is kept to a minimum. Governments can also take measures to support the growth of local contractors. This can be done not only by preferred treatment but also by putting money into training courses on financial management, administration and the most appropriate construction techniques. In the long term each developed country must have a viable domestic construction industry, whether public or private, for its own economic stability.

## 9. Summary

At the end of a fairly detailed coverage of the problems of the most appropriate technologies in road construction the overall problem of what are the required policy measures for large-scale implementation appears particularly broad. In general, however, what is required is a flexibility of approach, firm direction and support from the highest level and motivation for all concerned in the road construction process so that the most appropriate methods in terms of resource allocation are also the most efficient in the execution of projects.

**Notes and references**

[1] The author wishes to thank Dr. M. Allal and Mr. M.I. Hussain for their valuable comments during the preparation of this chapter. Dr. Allal's contributions on the economic aspects are gratefully acknowledged.

[2] *Study on the use of labour-intensive methods for the Indus Super Highway*, ILO Report to the Government of Pakistan, Chapter 6.

[3] ILO, "Implementation of appropriate road construction technology in Kenya", report of the joint Ministry of Works/ILO/NORAD project (mimeo.), Geneva, Nov. 1976.

[4] M. Allal and G.A. Edmonds, *Manual on the Planning of Labour-intensive Road Construction*, ILO, Geneva, 1977, Chapter 5.

[5] See W. McCleary et al, *Equipment versus employment: A social cost benefit analysis of alternative techniques of feeder road construction in Thailand*. ILO, Geneva, 1976, Appendix 2.

⁶ For a detailed discussion of this issue see M. Allal and G.A. Edmonds, op. cit., Chapter 8.

⁷ G.W. Irwin, et al. *Roads and Redistribution — Social Costs and Benefits of Labour-intensive Road Construction in Iran.* ILO, Geneva, 1975.

⁸ W.A. McCleary, et al. *Equipment versus Employment, op. cit.*

⁹ Deepak Lal, et al. *Men or Machines: A Philippines case study of labour-capital substitution in road construction*, ILO, Geneva, 1978.

¹⁰ *Manual on the Planning of Labour Intensive Road Construction, op. cit.*

¹¹ Report of the ILO/MOW/NORAD study, op. cit.

¹² Report of the ILO/MOW/NORAD study, op. cit.

¹³ An average figure would be of the order of 30 per cent.

¹⁴ See Manual, op. cit., Chapter 3.

¹⁵ Deepak Lal, et. al., op. cit.

¹⁶ Report of ILO/MOW/NORAD study, op. cit.

¹⁷ The example of the effective piece-rate system devised by the Chinese in Nepal is particularly relevant here. This is quoted in H. Rieger and B. Bhadra, "A comparative evaluation of road construction techniques in Nepal", Centre for Economic Development and Administration, Tribhuvhan University, Kathmandu, Aug. 1978.

¹⁸ R. Pilcher, *Principles of construction management*, McGraw-Hill, London, 1966.

¹⁹ R. Pilcher, *op. cit.*

²⁰ *Manual on the Planning of Labour-Intensive Construction, op. cit., Chapter 3.*

²¹ A recent study on appropriate technology in forestry operations in the Philippines was particularly successful in showing that efficient hand tools could considerably increase labour productivity. (See ILO, "Appropriate Technology in Philippine Forestry" (mimeo), ILO, October 1977).

²² The ILO is at present preparing a *Guide to Tools and Equipment for Labour-Based Road Construction*.

²³ Some reasons for this are presented in Chapter 4, which also suggests that the scope is considerably broader than thought at present.

²⁴ The ILO's Employment Mission to the Philippines in 1973 recommended that interest rates on lending should be increased to 17-18 per cent. This has since been done.

²⁵ This effect of wage subsidy payments was observed in Kenya during the ILO Employment Mission in 1972.

²⁶ *Roads and Redistribution, op. cit.*

²⁷ *Matching Employment Opportunities and Expectations: A Programme of Action for Ceylon.* Report and Technical Papers, ILO, Geneva, 1971.

²⁸ *Roads and Redistribution, op. cit.*

## CHAPTER 3. PLANNING AND ADMINISTRATION OF LABOUR-BASED ROAD CONSTRUCTION PROGRAMMES

*by B.E. Nilsson*

### 1. Introduction

The author has worked for several years with two of the projects that have contributed to this new way of looking at the matter, namely the Capas — Botolan project in the Philippines[1], and the Rural Access Roads Programme in Kenya[2]. While these two projects are good examples of the viability of labour-based methods they have also shown that it requires careful planning and foresight to make such projects successful. One must not be deceived into believing that the need for planning of labour-based work is less than that for equipment-based work. However, it is not always fully appreciated that the planning and administration of a labour-based project need to be approached in a somewhat different way than for an equipment-based project. Furthermore as there are yet very few engineers and managers with any substantial experience of labour-based methods in many countries it can be argued that a greater and more conscious effort has to be made when planning labour-based work.

In this chapter some of the most important aspects of the planning and administration[3] of labour-based work will be discussed. Much of the discussion is based on observations and lessons learned from the Kenya Rural Access Roads Programme. It is hoped that this programme will be a model for implementation elsewhere.

### 2. Programme planning

Let us assume that the public works department (PWD) of a certain country has taken the decision to execute a road construction programme using a technology appropriate to the country's labour-abundant economy. This does not mean that labour-based methods will be used indiscriminately but that serious and unbiased consideration should be given to how to carry out the various road construction activities so that the programme is compatible with the conditions and economy of that particular country. It also means that already at the design stage due consideration should be given to such aspects as standards, size of projects and construction time in order to avoid conditioning the choice of technology. However, as mentioned in the introduction, design will not be covered in this chapter and the discussions here thus assume that questions about standards and quality have been analysed without bias towards any particular technology.

## 2.1 Labour availability and costs

This has been discussed in detail in Chapter 2. Suffice it to say in addition that the cost of labour normally has an overriding influence on whether labour-based methods are economically justifiable or not. It is however not possible to give an exact "break-even" figure above which labour-based methods would be uneconomical because labour and machine productivity differ so much from country to country. Moreover, factors such as the type of project, its location, the availability of staff and (machine) service facilities play an important role. The question of whether to use market or "shadow" prices should also be noted. Market prices are easier to establish but it is generally accepted that shadow prices better reflect the "real" effect of using different technologies on a (developing) country's economy because market prices are often distorted in one way or another.

## 2.2 Selection of methods

If the conditions are generally favourable for labour-based methods one should examine to what degree it is feasible to use them. For a low-standard feeder road with small requirements on compaction and smoothness of the riding surface and not involving long-haul distances, all or nearly all activities can be done by labour. For a main road with high requirements on compaction and riding surface it would be difficult to achieve the required standards without using some kind of mechanical equipment. Nevertheless, clearing, earthworks and structures (which typically account for considerably more than half of the cost of a road project) can be done satisfactorily by labour. Thus, even on a main road it is feasible to use labour-based methods to a great extent if the economic conditions are favourable.

When deciding upon the optimum mix of labour and machines the planning engineer will have to go through the main activities and calculate the cost of each activity using either market prices or shadow prices. Obviously interdependent activities have to be regarded together to avoid mismatching and suboptimisation. Consider for example an excavation to fill operation where compaction by a mechanical roller is required to fulfil set standards. The excavating, loading, hauling, unloading and spreading activities may be most economically done by manual labour. Compaction however has to be done by a roller. Looking at the compaction activity alone it is likely that one would conclude that a large roller would give a lower cost per unit of output than a small roller. But the capacity of a large roller is so much greater than that of an ordinary earthwork gang that the roller would be idle most of the time thus greatly increasing compaction costs. A small roller could do the job equally well if the thickness of the layers was reduced and/or the number of passes was increased. Another advantage with the small roller would be that it could be moved more easily and thus be used at two or more adjacent fills. Another example is hauling over long distances. The hauling work may be least expensively done by large trucks. If, however, it is economical to do the loading by labour the long idle time of the truck during loading might make the use of trucks uneconomical. In such a case and over medium- to long-haul distances one tractor and two or more trailers might be economical as only the cheap component, the trailer, would be idle during loading. In countries where work animals are common these could also be extremely useful for short- to medium-haul distances.

The productivity and cost of resources need to be known when comparing different methods. A great deal of data is available on equipment-intensive techniques while comparatively little exists on labour-based techniques. A word of warning is however necessary regarding the use of cost and productivity data on machines. It is the experience of the author that when calculating hourly costs of machines, little consideration is given to low utilisation and idle time caused by less than ideal work planning and breakdowns.

At the same time productivity figures may be taken from manufacturers' handbooks which tend to be optimistic in general and reflect conditions in the land of manufacture, often an industrialised country. Taken together this can contribute to considerable underestimation of unit costs.

Labour productivity data may not be available to planning engineers in many PWDs. It is always advisable to use local data but if no systematically organised labour-based work of any scale has been done recently in the country, international sources can be used. The World Bank and the International Labour Organisation, among others, now have data from several parts of the world. Such data should however be used only for tentative planning and it should be the aim to establish local data as soon as possible[4].

## 2.3 *Time schedule*

Having made the choice of methods, a tentative time schedule should be drawn up. In the case of a large road project a bill of quantities will have been prepared. In the case of a feeder road programme only the approximate length of roads to be constructed may be known. In such a case an estimate of the quantities involved must be made. This can be done by classifying the different types of terrain encountered and estimating quantities per kilometer for each type of terrain. Knowing (or estimating) the number of kilometers in each type of terrain a tentative bill of quantities for the entire programme can be calculated.

When making the time schedule it must be borne in mind that the work may have to stop, or at least be reduced, during certain periods due to non-availability of labour or to unsuitable weather. However labour-intensive methods are less sensitive to rain than machine methods. If the rain periods are not too intensive in a particular region, labour-intensive work may be carried on with minimal interruption.

## 2.4 *Organisation and staff*

The time schedule should show the resources that would be needed at any given time. It must be checked carefully to ensure that it is possible to obtain the resources needed. Moreover, the level of resources required must be suitable from the technical point of view. For example, if too many labourers are crowded into one section of the road, productivity and economy will suffer. If the site is likely to become overcrowded the possibility of working simultaneously on more sites should be investigated. Where it is not possible to obtain the necessary resources, especially if there are shortages of supervisory staff, the time horizon of the programme would need to be lengthened.

If the road(s) to be built go through populated areas it is normally advantageous to employ labour who arrange their own transport to and from work. This is usually on foot and restricts the area from which labour can be drawn to 5-10 kms from the site. As the construction work progresses the distance to walk will be too great for the workers and new ones will have to be employed. The disadvantage with this system is that it takes a little time for the labourers to reach their full productivity. Thus, if the average length of employment is short, over-all productivity will suffer. The alternatives are to provide transport to the workers or to arrange labour camps. Both alternatives are costly and bring with them administrative and social problems. Therefore, if the turnover of labour can be kept to three to six months the slight loss in productivity incurred by employing new labour is generally preferable to the provision of transport or camps.

Naturally the organisation will depend on the size of the project and the type of the road(s). One proven organisation structure is to have one gang leader for every 20-25 workers and one foreman in charge of 3-4 gangs. The gang leader should be a worker who has the confidence of his fellows. He would leave the project when his gang terminates its employment, although the best gang leaders could be kept for training to become foremen. The foremen should be permanent or semi-permanent employees and kept throughout the project. Their technical skill need not be particularly high. In general, more consideration should be given to their ability to organise and motivate labourers. It is possible to train gangleaders with the right personal qualities to become foremen through comparatively short training courses. This is important because on large labour-intensive projects a great number of foremen are needed. Their performance is crucial to labour productivity and thereby also to the economy of the project.

For every two to four foremen (200-400 workers) a supervisor with good experience and knowledge of road construction would be needed. A technician with engineering training would be suitable for this post. He would be the man to solve most of the technical problems on projects consisting of many small and scattered sites.

Finally, there should be a roads engineer who could supervise two to three technicians and be assisted by supporting staff for surveying, accounting, supply and stores, work studies and other administrative matters.

The following number of supervisory staff would then be needed for a project employing about 1,000 workers:

1  Engineer
3  Technicians
10-12 Foremen
40-50 Gang leaders (casual employees)

It is emphasised that this is an example and that each project merits its own analysis of the need for staff. A project with many small sites will need more supervisory staff than a project with 1,000 workers at one site.

The demand for supporting staff is a function of the type of road and the size of sites. A high-standard main road will need a number of surveyors while a low-standard feeder road project might not need any surveyors at all. The supply function for a small site project will be more complicated than for a big site project. Each small site must have its own small store and a storeman (possibly a casual employee) which may serve only 100 workers, while the store at a big site might serve a much larger number of workers.

## 2.5 Training

Unless labour-based projects of some scale have been executed before in a country it is likely that the number of staff needed is not readily available. In that case training programmes must be set up before the start of the programme. If a big programme is envisaged the most suitable formula would be to start on a comparatively small scale (pilot project) for one or two years and during that time gain experience of the type of training that is needed and the most appropriate way to carry it out. If the programme will ultimately employ a very large labour-force, say in the order of tens of thousands, a build-up over several years will be required and training will be continuous.

It is likely that the training need is most crucial at the level of site foremen. It is extremely important that they be fully competent in the work methods to be used, as they will give the daily instructions on site and train the gang leaders and the workers. They can be recruited from the level of gang leaders provided they have a sound knowledge of basic arithmetic and an understanding of simple planning and reporting. Above all, they must have an aptitude for man management.

Training courses might also be needed for the technicians and engineers and possibly also for drivers, operators and mechanics if some equipment is to be used.

The emphasis of the training should be on field work. In many PWDs there are staff training departments where a special branch could be created to carry out the necessary training for labour-based projects. The management of a project should be ultimately responsible for the training but not for the day-to-day running of it. It is recommended that the training branch be given a special field unit where they can plan the construction work according to the training needs.

Ideally, instruction and training manuals should be written for the programme. Existing handbooks can be useful but do not reduce the need for manuals specific to the programme. These should deal with administrative routines, work methods and organisation, planning and reporting procedures as well as productivity, cost and production targets and resource allocation. The best way of using existing "universal" manuals is to extract and amend certain sections of them to suit specific country and programme conditions.

Feedback from field units to the training branch is very important. Some form of periodic review of the training course should be carried out between all the involved parties, i.e. the programme headquarters, the field personnel and the training branch. At these reviews certain questions should be examined. These would include the effectiveness of the training (whether the trainees know and can apply what they have been taught), the relevance of the syllabuses to the field requirements and whether the methods taught correspond to actual, practical field procedures.

Gang leaders and workers and also some of the administrative staff would not be subject to any formalised training. In their case on-the-job training will be of great importance. It is absolutely essential that all levels of supervisors are made aware of this. This sort of informal training is done in the course of their daily duties and should take the form of both instructions and practical demonstrations. It should be followed up by control and repetitions if necessary.

Labour-based work carries relatively little "status" and it is therefore particularly important to promote interest in training and in the daily work by offering promotion possibilities. In a new and growing programme there is fortunately a good chance for this. However, promotion should be given on merit and not based only on years of service. Persons participating in courses should know that if they have performed well they will stand a good chance of being promoted. Care must therefore be exercised when selecting people for courses. The potential trainee's performance in his present job is of course important. Even more essential however is the assessment of how he would perform in his next job which might require different personal qualities.

## 2.6 *Tools and equipment*

The general aspects of tools and equipment have been discussed in Chapter 2. However, as far as specific programmes are concerned planners should investigate the whole range of questions related to tools at least one year before the intended start of a programme. The first important issue is to decide broadly which work methods are going to be used. Knowing that and the parameters such as soil types, it is then possible to decide the types of tool to be used and to make a rough estimate of the numbers needed. The number needed of each type of tool is dependent on the quantity of each activity, the number of workers and the parameters and the quality of the tools. Spare tools and handles must also be provided for.

When types, specifications and numbers of tools have been decided a survey of the local market has to be carried out. If the desired tools are available on the local market, laboratory tests and also, if possible, field tests, should be carried out. If the tools are not available or if they fail the tests it might be possible to get local factories to take up new products and/or to improve the quality of their existing range of products. If this is not possible preparations for importation of tools have to be made.

It is usually economic to repair or recycle tools, for example, to weld a new blade to a hoe, a new prong to a fork or reforging a pickaxe. For this, a small workshop equipped with an electric arc-welding machine, a grinding machine, a forge and a couple of anvils and vices, etc., is needed.

As stated above, the selection of work methods governs the requirement for tools and equipment. If for example work animals are going to be used there will probably be a need for rippers, scrapers and various types of cart. Again agricultural-type implements may not be suitable and efforts may be needed to develop and manufacture better ones. A lot of development work has however been done by various organisations in several countries and by consulting them development work will not have to start from scratch.

## 2.7 Budget

At this stage a tentative budget can be made. The assessment of costs of resources in terms of labour, staff, material, tools and equipment, including running costs, camps, offices and related overheads is comparatively straightforward once input/output relationships are established and methods chosen. The cost of training facilities, management and planning staff at headquarters and method study personnel is more difficult to estimate but should not be forgotten. To a large extent the cost of these items depends on whether existing facilities and procedures are suitable for a labour-based programme or not. It is extremely important to examine this aspect in detail before the start of a programme. A thorough analysis should be done of how existing routines need to be modified by someone familiar with labour-based work. This must commence well in advance, at least a half to one year before the intended start of a programme. The time and money spent on this will certainly pay off in terms of reduced disruptions and delays. Nevertheless, if labour-based work on a big scale is completely new to a PWD, adjustments of administrative routines and the organisational structure may have to be done after the start of a project even though considerable time has been spent on this in advance. The productivity of labour and estimates of quantities and material will also be subject to correction when experience has been gained. It is therefore natural that, unless the PWD has recent extensive experience of labour-based programmes, the tentative budget may be a best estimate only.

The tentative budget is of course of utmost importance for the financial negotiations for the project. It seems that both bilateral and multilateral development agencies look favourably upon labour-based projects. A sound budget for a well-planned programme is a valuable asset in such negotiations.

## 3. Administration — policy and procedures

If a PWD has not earlier employed large numbers of casual labour there would be a need to establish a labour and staff policy for the project. The changes or amendments to administrative procedures may also be so far-reaching that it is worth setting up new administrative policies.

### 3.1 *Labour policy*

Most PWDs, being part of a country's civil service, employ their labour, including unskilled labour, on a permanent or semi-permanent basis. Consequently existing codes and regulations do not fit a situation where casual labour is employed on a large scale. A new set of regulations may have to be created. As far as possible this should be done before the start of a project and in consultation with the Ministry of Labour to avoid disputes regarding the terms of employment.

a) *Wages*[5] — If there is a legal minimum wage this will often be the actual wage paid to the workers. An exception might have to be made if the wage for casual labour in, for example agriculture, is higher than the minimum wage. In a country with large unemployment this would probably only happen in certain regions or seasons unless the minimum wage regulations are very old. If wages lower than the minimum wage are common for casual agricultural work the minimum wage has to be used for budgeting purposes whilst a shadow wage could be used when choosing technology. Care must be taken that road construction does not disrupt agricultural production in an area.

This could happen if the wages paid to road workers were higher than agricultural wages and the labour supply insufficient for both activities during peak agricultural seasons.

Payment in kind, i.e. when a certain portion of the wages is paid not in cash but, for example, as foodstuff, has been tried from time to time. If a large portion of the wage is paid in kind it seems that the workers look upon their job as a kind of welfare programme and motivation is often lacking. Payment in kind is also administratively burdensome and the author's opinion is that it should be avoided[6].

The pay period should if possible be one month. Shorter pay periods require more administrative work and greater loss of working time. Local practice may however require shorter pay periods. Daily payment is unsuitable for large-scale projects.

b) *Working time*[7] — Manual road construction work is arduous and in a hot climate it is not possible to keep a high output over eight hours. To avoid the worst heat, work should preferably start early in the morning, break for several hours around noon and continue in mid-afternoon. This is not always easy to arrange but should be aimed at where feasible. If work animals are used they often set their own pace which man has to follow whether he likes it or not.

Rules about remuneration when work cannot be carried out, for example, due to inclement weather, should be included in the terms of employment.

c) *Social benefits and security*[8] — The nature of casual employment implies that the workers will have to be dismissed after the completion of a project, subproject or a certain stretch of road. This procedure, however, must be compatible with the labour legislation in the country. Some countries have labour laws which automatically make employment permanent after a certain period of time. However desirable from the social point of view, it may in some circumstances completely defeat the idea of labour-based work which in many cases is tied to the concept of temporary employment.

Other questions on social security concern sickness and accidents. If the labourers are to be paid for days when they are sick what kind of control should be implemented? Will the PWD be responsible for accident during work and if so to what extent? Should social security charges (if applicable) be deducted from the wages or covered by the PWD?

d) *Incentives* — If labour-based work is to be economically viable it is fundamental to keep a high labour productivity. To achieve this it is important that the workers feel that their job is meaningful. If they live near the road to be constructed they normally feel well motivated as the road will serve them when completed. The workers should also feel that they are not unfairly treated and that their terms of employment and working conditions are reasonable.

Some form of incentive payment scheme can raise productivity considerably. The obvious method is piecework, i.e. the worker is paid for each unit of output. The harder he works, the more money he gets. Another method is taskwork. Taskwork means that a worker, or more often a gang of workers, gets a task to finish in a certain period of time (often one day but it can be longer). When the gang has completed the task satisfactorily the labourers are free to go home still earning a full day's pay. The incentive is not that they can earn more money, as in piecework, but they can get more spare time to use as they please, e.g. for work on their farms. Piecework and taskwork can increase productivity by 50 per cent or more compared with non-incentive timework (i.e. daily paid without any set task).

Piecework usually yields somewhat higher productivity than taskwork but is not always more economical because it is more burdensome and costly to administer. For small sites where no bill of quantities is made and little or no surveyor assistance is available taskwork is recommended. For large roads these facilities are usually provided and piecework can be introduced for many of the main activities. Before either is introduced a good knowledge of labour productivity must be obtained through work studies to prevent large changes in the set rates. A policy should also be established on action to be taken if the workers fail to finish a task during normal working hours and whether workers on piecework should be allowed to work longer days in order to earn more.

e) *Tools, equipment, work animals* — In this regard responsibility of the employer and the employees should be laid down. Tools and equipment are preferably provided by the employer and the worker's responsibility in case of loss should be agreed upon. Work animals on the other hand need care and food even after working hours and would be a burden for the site management to own or keep. It is therefore preferable to hire work animals with a driver. In the agreement the responsibility of both the owner/driver and the employer (particularly in case of illness, accidents or death) should be spelt out.

## 3.2 *Staff policy*

The staff requirements for labour-based work are different from those of capital-intensive work. The latter requires fewer supervisors and most of them need a good technical education. The execution of labour-based work requires more supervisory staff but many of them need comparatively little technical education. As capital-intensive methods in many countries are the prevalent way of constructing roads, staff regulations are naturally geared towards their use with emphasis on academic qualifications. For labour-based work, supervisors need to have man-management and organisational abilities rather than sophisticated technical training. This does not mean that their work carries little responsibility. On the contrary they often have to work quite independently at a fairly low level in the hierarchy. A foreman at a small site project is commonly alone on an isolated site and has to do the daily planning, reporting, instruction and supervision by himself. The problem is that government regulations often do not recognise that persons with little formal education can take on this kind of responsibility and therefore their employment and promotion will be difficult to accomplish. If a government wants to carry out labour-based work it must accept the different requirements and make it possible to employ and keep the type of personnel needed.

In this context it can also be pointed out that existing rules for housing and field allowances and overtime should be examined to see if they are applicable and relevant to a situation which may not have been foreseen.

## 3.3 *Distribution*

The distribution of supplies of tools should not be a problem if the project consists of only a few large sites. Each site would then have its own store facilities and possibly also the authorisation to buy small quantities of tools directly. With many small sites it is quite a different matter. It would be uneconomical to store large quantities of every item which may be needed at each site. The only solution seems to be very careful planning and the establishment of depots in various parts of the country, each of them serving a number of sites. The importance of a good distribution system is frequently overlooked although the lack of tools, spares or material is a major bottleneck on many construction sites whether they are capital intensive or use labour-based methods.

## 3.4 *Payment of wages*

It is extremely important that the workers get paid on time. Hardly anything lowers the morale of the labour force as much as delayed pay. Most PWDs have no experience of paying very large numbers of workers in the field and scattered all over the country. This must therefore be given careful consideration and, if necessary, new routines created. To ensure punctuality the system should be decentralised as far as the calculation of wages and payment is concerned. Necessary checks and auditing would of course be done afterwards at headquarters.

A system along the following lines would have a good chance of functioning properly. The engineer requests well in advance of pay day that the approximate amount of money needed (not to be underestimated) be paid to a local bank from headquarters. The men who keep the muster rolls, normally the foremen, send them to the engineer one week before pay day covering the period from one week before last pay day to one week before this pay day. The individual wages are then calculated at the engineer's office. The engineer should personally make the payment on at least one site per month (not known which in advance) as a precaution against fraud. Another check that should be done at irregular intervals during the month is that the number of workers present at the site corresponds with the number on the muster roll that particular day.

The above system requires that the engineer is given authority which he may not enjoy according to existing regulations. It is however difficult to run a programme of widely spread small sites without giving a large amount of authority to field officers.

## 4. Site management

### 4.1 *Organising the work*

Before any large number of workers is employed offices, store and tools should be furnished. The alignment also needs to be established for the first part of the road. On a high-standard road this would be done by a surveyor in the conventional way according to drawings provided. On a low-standard road the alignment might be decided on the spot. The technician (referred to in the organisation previously outlined) should be able to do that assisted by the foreman but might, in complicated cases, take advice from the engineer. When the centre line is set out the foreman can set out road width, ditches and cut levels together with his gang leaders.

The recruitment of labour can be done in various ways. The easiest way is to ask a local chief, community leader or barrio captain to organise it. Another method is to let it be known that labour will be employed on a certain day and if the number arriving is greater than needed, make the selection by drawing of lots. The latter method eliminates, or at least reduces, the possibility that somebody draws unfair advantages from the recruitment situation.

As both labourers and gang leaders are casual employees they will know little about the work to begin with. It will be up to the foreman to instruct them, a task which initially will take much of his time. It is therefore desirable to have a staggered start to the work. Each foreman should engage a new gang with at least two or three days interval. This also contributes to good work sequencing. The first gang would do bush clearing, the second gang removal of topsoil, the third gang excavation, etc. Depending on quantities involved two or three gangs would be needed for one task and maybe only half a gang for another. The aim is to get an even progress of the work so that each task is sufficiently well ahead of the following task without getting so far in advance that supervision becomes difficult. The above applies also to large sites with the exception that each foreman would specialise in one task and all his gangs would do the same task. At the gang level a specialisation is desirable, regardless of size of site, to improve productivity.

It is important, but often neglected, to teach the labourers efficient work methods. Take, as an example, the excavation of soil from one side of the road to be used as fill on the other side. Often workers move the soil three or four times, about one meter at a time, instead of throwing it across the road in one throw. For a given amount of soil the latter method is quicker and less fatiguing. Other examples are to place a wheelbarrow in the right place and position to ease loading, to see that the runway for a wheelbarrow is smooth and hard, to circulate activities within a gang in order to distribute the most strenuous work. These are all small details but taken together they will have a major impact on productivity and considerably facilitate the work for the labourers.

The importance of incentive systems has been stressed earlier. It is obvious that a decrease in the pay per unit of output (for piecework) or an increase in the daily task (for taskwork) will not be popular among the workers. This implies that the pay per unit should be kept on the low side and the daily task on the high side to start with if there is uncertainty about what rates to set. The idea being that any change would be favourable to the workers and therefore not meet with resistance. But if the pay appears too low or the task too big the workers would not feel motivated and the experiment be useless. This is a delicate situation and the best thing to do when uncertain is to work on a timework basis for some time while studying productivity. This should preferably be done in a way that enables measurement of work periods and rest periods to assess whether the pace of work is reasonable or not.

## 4.2 *Planning*

When planning construction work it must be remembered that the hourly or daily productivity is not the same as long-term productivity. The former is what can be achieved when work progresses more or less uninterrupted while the latter indicates what can be expected over longer periods — a month or a season. Over such periods disturbances are bound to occur and cause idle time whether the work is executed by labour or machines. One purpose of planning is to minimise idle time.

A frequent reason for delays is inclement weather. However, this follows a yearly pattern and consideration of this must be taken in the plans. Breakdowns are another common reason for work stoppages on equipment-intensive work. The equivalent of this in labour-based works would be labour absenteeism or shortages. Labour supply estimates, particularly in respect of differences between agricultural off seasons and peak seasons, can however minimise problems of this nature.

The relationship between long-term productivity and daily productivity thus depends on factors such as the quality of planning, the weather and "breakdowns" taken in a wide sense to include such things as labour shortages. Daily productivity can be assessed relatively quickly through work studies. Only experience over a long time, however, can give the frequency of work disruptions and hence the long-term productivity. Good planning, including consideration of the weather and the study of the labour supply, can however bring the two concepts close to each other in value.

The planning techniques which can be used differ depending on the type and size of road. For a big main road project the same well-known techniques as for capital-intensive jobs can be used, for example, bar chart, time and location chart or the critical path method. More detailed planning will however be necessary, as the standard unit of input, a gang of labour, has an output which is only a fraction of that of a big machine. It is desirable to have at least two levels of plan. There should be at one level an over-all plan stating in general terms the expected progress and needed resources over the life of the project. The other plan, drawn up fortnightly or monthly, would detail where and in what numbers each resource (labour, equipment, material) would be needed and the expected output.

At a small site the planning has to be simplified. Often there is a lack of most or all of the needed facilities such as drawings, bills of quantities, surveyors and most of all a person familiar with sophisticated planning techniques. The foreman would normally do the short-term planning which probably would extend over a few days or possibly up to one week. A simple form listing the common activities with the number of workers and the chainage for the actual activities would be an adequate format for this planning. Volumes of excavation in bulk could be estimated by the "slotting techniques". This means that a vertical slot, perpendicular to the direction of the road should be excavated to the intended level of cut. The slot would be as wide as is convenient to excavate and extend to the intended backslope of the road. The height and width of the cut can then be measured without using any instrument and the volume calculated by the foremen in order to set appropriate tasks. This method is well suited only for sidecuts and not for "full" cuts but these are unusual on low-standard roads.

Small sites may not need a comprehensive bill of quantities. However, an estimate of the quantities of the major activities is desirable in order to make a rough plan for the whole road and to have something with which to compare input of resources. A technician trained and experienced in estimating quantities could do this work. He would walk along the road and estimate the density of bush, the approximate height of cuts and relevant parameters such as soil class, location of culverts and bridges, etc. If the same person made the estimate on all roads it would be sufficiently reliable for simple planning and control of efficiency.

The yearly construction programme for simple rural roads has to be based more upon judgement of the terrain types than upon actual estimates.

### 4.3 *Reporting and control*

Planning is aimed at getting the right resource in the right numbers at the right place at the right time. To be useful the planning has to be updated regularly in relation to the present situation and recent experience. Therefore the progress and the use of resources must be controlled. The control process will take place at all levels of the organisation hierarchy and, to enable this, a flow of reports must be established. A good reporting system is particularly essential in a programme with many small sites as the project management cannot visit each site often. As one moves up the hierarchy of reports, they must be more and more condensed. The project manager would obviously not have time to go through detailed reports from a large number of sites but must have them in a form which quickly tells him the status of the programme.

The reporting starts from the foreman level with a daily report of input in terms of labour, equipment and material. This is fairly simple and should be standardised. The reporting of output is more complicated and the format may vary depending on conditions. If there is a reliable bill of quantities, reporting of chainage or station number is meaningful as it can be translated into quantities. If there is no bill of quantities less direct methods of measurement have to be employed. If task work or piecework has been used quantities for at least the major activities must have been estimated and should be reported. Where no exact and comprehensive measurement of quantities has been done the roads should be grouped into classes related to their degree of difficulty of construction. This could be based on the rough estimate done by the engineer's assistant mentioned earlier. A division into four or five classes would be sufficient to help judge whether the number of man-days used and the incurred costs are reasonable or not for the actual road. Due consideration must of course be given to large structures or other non-typical items.

The foreman should summarise his daily reports into a monthly report. This should go to the next level in the hierarchy which earlier has been called the technician. After having checked his foreman's reports they would be summarised and the technician's own costs added. These would consist of his own staff costs and overheads and transportation and various items which the foreman cannot easily price, for example, material or the use of equipment. Depending on conditions such as the availability of clerical staff the calculation of costs and summary of reports could alternatively be done at the engineer's office where of course his overheads should also be added.

The engineer should submit monthly reports to the project manager (headquarters). As a minimum these should contain:
— projects started, on-going and finished;
— progress in kilometers for different classes of roads;
— average costs and input of man-days per kilometer for different classes of roads;
— average costs and inputs of man-days per unit of output for different activities (where quantities are measured);
— breakdown of expenditure into labour wages, staff wages, equipment costs, tools, materials and camp and office costs;
— costs, type and sizes of structures;
— staff situation;
— total number of casual employees and worked man-days;

- utilisation of vehicles and equipment.

The control and reporting system should serve as an indication to supervisors at all levels whether his unit is functioning well or not. It can also be used as a feed-back system to continuously obtain more reliable data for planning at all levels and to improve fair piecework and taskwork rates.

## 5. Conclusions

It is not possible to simplify the planning and administration process by saying that there is one solution for capital-intensive work and another for labour-based work. Procedures and regulations are not the same in all countries and this has to be respected. Moreover, it is not possible or desirable to completely change the pattern of work within a PWD when introducing labour-based methods. Nevertheless, modifications and adjustments will be needed. For a programme to have any chance of success will depend on the possibility of making these changes or, in other words, the seriousness of the government's commitment.

The type and the size of the project is of great importance for planning and administration. A low-standard road project often consists of many small sites where each site, of necessity, will have limited staff and facilities. This obviously calls for other procedures than for the construction of main roads because there the technical requirements are higher, the sites are normally bigger and more labour and staff are involved at each site.

If the PWD has little or no previous experience of labour-based work the planning process must start well in advance of the construction of roads. The supply of labour must be analysed, particularly in respect of seasonal and regional variations. The role of the middle-management staff is crucial and some form of training will be necessary. It has to be recognised however that formal education is less important than man-management ability for most of the supervisory staff. Both staff policy and labour policy must be open to reconsideration. Because so many people are involved, standardised and formalised routines are indispensable.

The problems have to be identified and solved in each individual case and country. Engineers and administrators must take the decisions and responsibilities. Nevertheless, persons with experience of similar types of projects from other countries can be of help in identifying problem areas before the problems arise and indicate solutions which have been effective elsewhere.

**Notes and references**

[1] Capas — Botolan is a main highway project about 100 kms north of Manila. A 6 km section of it was built as a pilot project using labour-based methods in 1974. It employed some 800 labourers and a large number of work animals. This is described in Deepak Lal, *Men or Machines: A study of labour-capital substitution in road construction in the Philippines*. ILO, Geneva, 1978.

[2] The Rural Access Roads Programme involves the construction of some 14,000 kms of minor roads in rural areas all over Kenya using labour-based methods. It started in 1974 and by the end of 1977 about 2,000 casual workers were employed. It is finally expected to employ about 20,000 workers and be completed by 1983. (See MOW/ILO/NORAD report, op. cit., and ILO, *The Rural Access Roads Programme, Kenya*, forthcoming publication.)

[3] The concept of planning and administration is here used in a rather wide sense although some facets of it, notably technical design, are excluded.

[4] See World Bank/ILO. *Programme Planning and Management Handbook*. Forthcoming publication.

[5] Various aspects of the payment of wages are covered under the Protection of Wages Convention, 1949, adopted by the International Labour Conference.

[6] Payment in kind is dealt with under the Protection of Wages Convention, 1949, adopted by the International Labour Conference. Inter alia, this restricts payment in kind to not more than 50 per cent of the total wage. This applies only to those people to whom wages are paid or payable.

[7] The recommended working week is 40 hours as laid down in the Reduction of Hours of Work (Public Works) Convention, 1936, adopted by the International Labour Conference.

[8] Questions related to the safety and health of workers have been dealt with in the ILO "Code of practice on safety and health in building and civil engineering work", ILO, Geneva, 1972. Questions related to accommodation and welfare facilities for workers have been dealt with in the Welfare Facilities Recommendation, 1956, and in the Workers' Housing Recommendation adopted by the International Labour Conference.

## CHAPTER 4. EQUIPMENT FOR LABOUR-BASED ROAD CONSTRUCTION

*by J.D.G.F. Howe and I. Barwell*

### 1. Introduction

The efficiency of mechanised road construction methods has improved continuously because the manufacturers of plant and equipment, the main elements of production, have developed new and better machines which reduce construction costs and raise productivity. The main elements of production in labour-based road construction are the hand tools and simple items of equipment used. Yet, in those countries where labour-based methods are used there has been little effort made to improve the design of existing implements or to introduce new, simple techniques. This contrast was highlighted by ESCAP[1] 20 years ago when they described earthwork by manual labour as an ancient art in which there had been little or no progress in the techniques used. On the other hand they noted that mechanised earthwork, which is of comparatively recent origin, had made rapid strides because plant and equipment had been and are constantly being improved.

The scant attention paid to the implements used in labour-based road construction is difficult to explain fully, but two possible factors are worth highlighting:
  i) while the implements are the *main* elements of production they are a very *minor* element of the construction *budget* and therefore their significance tends to be overlooked;
  ii) the implements used are generally the traditional tools of the society undertaking the work and their familiarity means that the possibility of change or improvement is not considered.

The paucity of effort expended on developing appropriate

equipment for labour-based road construction is in itself a compelling reason for believing the potential for improvement to be virtually untapped. This contention is supported by the recent studies of the ILO and the IBRD to establish the limit to which labour can be substituted for equipment in road construction. Amongst the significant conclusions to emerge from these studies are:
  i) that traditional labour-intensive civil works are inefficient and economically inferior to capital-intensive works, except at extremely low wage levels;
  ii) that a major cause of the inefficiency of traditional labour-based methods is simply that the tools, equipment, techniques and organisation are invariably primitive; and
  iii) that there exists a *range* of technically and economically feasible methods — varying from the most labour-intensive through *intermediate* techniques to the most equipment-intensive — depending upon the circumstances of the site and the application of superior tools, high incentives and good management.

The fact that the primitive nature of the technology has a limiting effect on efficiency is crucial because arguably it is the starting point in a series of events that at present condemn traditional labour-based methods.

Austen[2] speaks of:

> The vicious circle of primitive technology leading to low productivity leading to low wages leading back to primitive technology because we cannot afford to pay higher wages.

Two other elements could be introduced into the circle. Low wages leading to *"poor motivation"* — which accentuates the low productivity due to the primitive technology — and low productivity leading to *"the economic uncompetitiveness of labour with capital equipment"*. The wider use of more appropriate construction technologies that utilise wherever possible the labour resources most developing countries possess in abundance will clearly depend upon this circle being broken in as many places as possible. Improvements to tools and equipment is certainly a sensible starting point.

There are, however, formidable obstacles to be overcome. It is sobering to note that while gains in productivity from improved tools and equipment have been demonstrated

experimentally, there is little evidence that such improvements are being widely applied in practice. There are a number of reasons for this:
  i) there is, unfortunately, no professional prestige in organising unemployed manpower: the glamour lies in the employment of sophisticated equipment. That this sentiment is widespread is undeniable, but why and what to do about it? Clearly there are many psychological reasons connected with the status and image of the engineer in the eyes of society at large and of his professional colleagues. If that is the case, there is reason for optimism in the changing attitudes towards more appropriate technologies that can be discerned world-wide;
  ii) more specifically, present indifference by the engineer towards labour-based methods is perhaps because the *need for good quality, well-designed tools and equipment*, the *scope for using intermediate technologies* and the *inherent technical challenges* are not appreciated;
  iii) there is no commercial pressure group to stimulate the development and use of new and better simple implements, in contrast to the situation that exists in the case of large, mechanised road construction equipment;
  iv) in many developing countries the capability of local manufacturers to produce good quality, efficient implements is limited;
  v) even where the capability exists, local manufacturers may be unwilling to take the financial risks involved in producing new or improved implements because there is a lack of proof of demand.

Attention to the design of existing tools is only one part of the problem of improving the technology of labour-based road construction. In most developing countries road construction practice remains highly labour intensive or highly capital intensive. Little use is made of intermediate techniques which are designed to be labour intensive, but incorporate some capital outlay on light equipment so as to improve technical or economic efficiency. The most promising future for labour-based road construction may well lie in the widespread adoption of these intermediate technologies.

## Table 1: Available construction methods

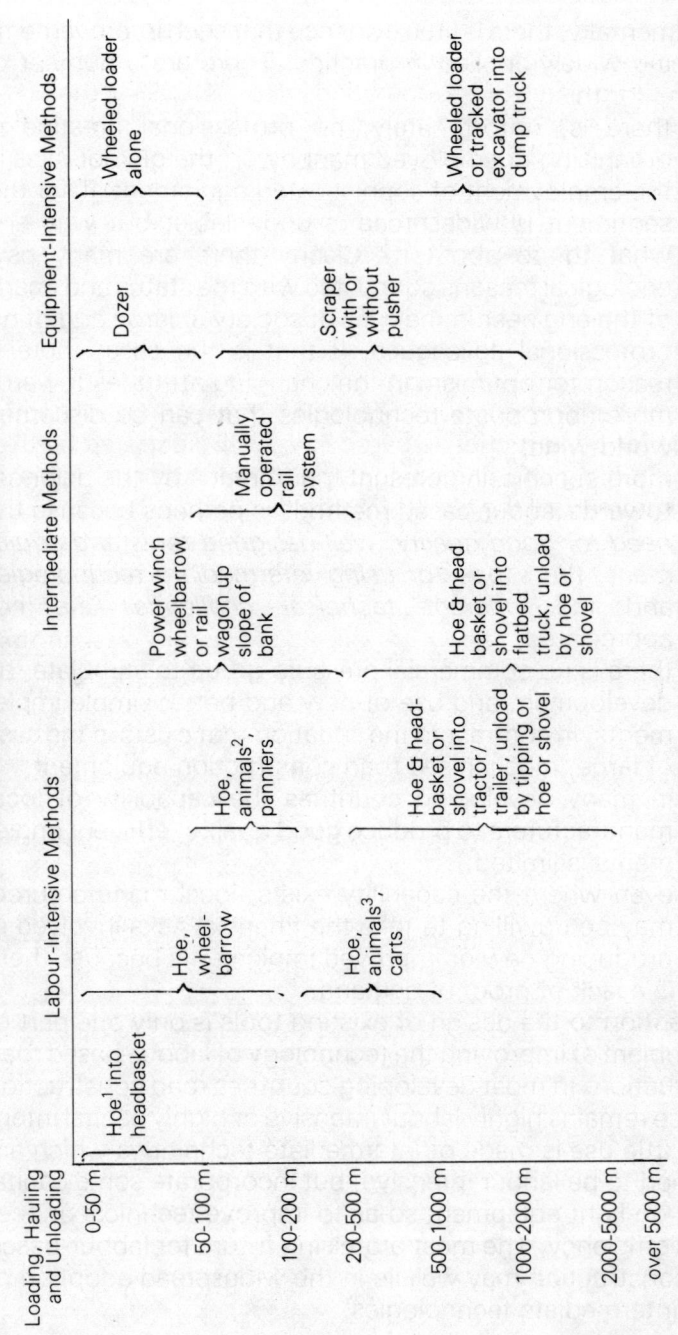

| Loading, Hauling and Unloading | Labour-Intensive Methods | | Intermediate Methods | | Equipment-Intensive Methods | |
|---|---|---|---|---|---|---|
| 0-50 m | Hoe[1] into headbasket | | | | Wheeled loader alone | |
| 50-100 m | | Hoe, wheel-barrow | | | | |
| 100-200 m | | | Power winch wheelbarrow or rail wagon up slope of bank | | Dozer | |
| 200-500 m | | Hoe, animals[2], panniers | | | | |
| 500-1000 m | | | Hoe & head-basket or shovel into tractor/trailer, unload by tipping or hoe or shovel | Manually operated rail system | | Wheeled loader or tracked excavator into dump truck |
| 1000-2000 m | | | | | | |
| 2000-5000 m | | Hoe, animals[3], carts | Hoe & head basket or shovel into flatbed truck, unload by hoe or shovel | | Scraper with or without pusher | |
| over 5000 m | | | | | | |

Notes:
[1] The word 'hoe' is used in the study to describe the back-acting tool used for digging in soft soil and for loading, variously named 'powrah', 'mamti', etc.
[2] i.e. mule, donkey or camel.
[3] i.e. mule, camel or bullock.

The purpose of this chapter is to demonstrate the potential for intermediate techniques in labour-based road construction by focusing on earthwork operations and discussing the possibilities for developing some of the simple equipment currently used and for introducing new types of equipment. While the chapter is specifically concerned with earthworks this aspect of road building has been chosen simply as a means of illustrating the wider potential for intermediate techniques and the conclusions drawn can be applied equally to other road construction operations.

## 2. **Equipment and earthmoving**

The technical and economic feasibility of a range of technologies for construction is particularly well illustrated by the loading, hauling and unloading cycle for earthworks. Table 1 gives a summary of the results from recent World Bank studies in India and Indonesia[3]. For the purposes of this discussion there are two noteworthy aspects. First, the list of methods experimented with is not exhaustive and there are notable omissions. Second, there is a close correlation between the preferred construction method and the length of haul. From these observations and a detailed study of the experimental work on equipment it is possible to put forward two propositions that will form the basis of subsequent discussions.

First, that there remains considerable scope for improving existing methods and further gains in productivity and/or the haul range over which they are technically and economically feasible could be realised.

Second, that there already exist — generally outside the labour-abundant countries, either as working units in non-construction activities or as prototypes — a number of *other* possible innovative means for moving earth that could probably extend still further the choice for the engineer of technically and economically feasible construction methods.

In civil construction the current choice of earthmoving modes is much more limited than the diverse range of devices available for the transport of general goods. This observation is important since in civil construction hauling is fundamentally a transport operation, though it has certain specific characteristics:

i)  the equipment is used very intensively in arduous conditions, and therefore needs to be ruggedly constructed if it is to be reliable and have a long life;
ii) the loading and unloading elements of the earthmoving cycle are critical in terms of maximising productivity and equipment utilisation.

Thus, while the principles of many of the devices currently used for goods transport can *potentially* be applied to haulage in civil construction, they will need to be adapted to the specific characteristics of this activity, if they are to be used with success. Discussion will be limited to methods which in table 1 are broadly classified as either labour-intensive or intermediate, lying between the headbasket and the flat-bed truck.

The headbasket is probably the supreme example of appropriate technology in road construction. It is simple, can be very cheap if made from local materials, and for certain tasks is as near optimum as any other method, e.g. very short hauls of 30 m or less, particularly on difficult terrain, and for the excavation and spoilage of material from deep culvert trenches. It offers little scope for improvement other than to find ways of introducing it to the many areas where it is not at present used. Two problems have to be combatted. First, lack of knowledge about the techniques and materials for making baskets, and the organisation and execution of work when they are used. Second, prejudice about the carrying of loads on the head, which is the case in parts of Africa, the Caribbean and Central South America. There are several sources of information about the first of these problems[4,5], whilst the second might best be overcome by a combination of education, demonstration and incentives.

Although table 1 classifies flat-bed trucks as an intermediate method of haulage this must surely be in an opportunistic sense only. If the facility is not being employed for the transport of conventional goods then it might be worthwhile to use it for relatively long-distance haulage. However, it can rarely be the optimum technological choice since as an expensive capital asset it cannot be economic to have it idle whilst it is being loaded and unloaded. The latter operation, particularly, is inherently slow. There seems to be little justification for trying to improve flat-bed trucks for earth haulage: better to develop more appropriate alternatives.

The technical options which follow are considered in order of their increasing power output: human, animal and engine.

## 3. Human

All labour-based methods of moving material require a somewhat different approach to the design of roads from that usual when equipment-intensive means are used. *This point cannot be over-emphasised as it is one of the most common misunderstandings*. Fundamentally labour-based methods require that haul distances be minimised wherever possible. Fortunately in most developing countries the borrowing and tipping of soil adjacent to the road is the normal practice rather than the balancing of cuts and fills along the length of the road which is usual with capital-intensive construction. The minimisation of haul distances is of course especially important for all human powered methods of haulage.

*Wheelbarrows*. Potentially the wheelbarrow is probably the single most useful item of equipment for labour-based road construction. For haul lengths of greater than about 20 m-30 m the use of wheelbarrows or handcarts increases the productivity of labour in earthmoving tasks compared with head, back or shoulder loading since the energy of labour is used much more efficiently.

A conventional wheelbarrow has a single wheel of fairly small diameter (up to 400 mm) positioned in front of the load pan. The single-wheeled barrow is superior to a two-wheeled handcart, primarily because, on the rough ground which prevails on construction sites, a cart is likely to be diverted from its direction of travel every time one wheel hits a bump, pothole or rock. However, many of the wheelbarrows commonly in use are of an extremely inefficient design and are poorly manufactured.

Perhaps the oldest of modern attempts at improved wheelbarrow design is to be found in the ILO Study, *Men who Move Mountains*[6]. It is surprising that the excellent work in this study has found little appreciation even among subsequent experimental investigators, much less so in practice. More recently the World Bank has initiated detailed investigative work on the use of wheelbarrows for haulage[7,8,9]. From these and other studies general design principles have been evolved.

For optimum performance of the wheelbarrow, resistance

to motion must be minimised, and this implies efficient bearings, maintenance of the haul route in good condition, and the use of a wheel with low-rolling resistance. (In this context a pneumatic tyre is beneficial and performance is improved by using a large diameter wheel.) Wheelbarrows must be very sturdily constructed to have a useful working life in the arduous conditions of a construction site.

Because of its low power-to-weight ratio, a loaded wheelbarrow pushed by a single person cannot normally operate on uphill gradients greater than about 6 per cent (World Bank) though short, steeper slopes can be negotiated by taking a run and using the momentum of the wheel to ascend the incline. For longer, steep slopes, assisted haulage can be used either by multi-person operation on the gradient, or by employing a winch. The latter practice was commonplace in the construction of railways and canals in Europe in the last century, although as then executed, using horse-powered winches, it was considered to be dangerous[10].

*The Chinese Wheelbarrow.* The wheelbarrow used in China has developed quite independently and differs from the conventional configuration in three fundamental ways[11,12]:

i) it uses a large diameter wheel and consequently has a very low rolling resistance. Traditional Chinese wheelbarrows had solid or spoked wooden wheels approximately 1 m in diameter[13]; Contemporary versions use a pneumatically tyred, tension-spoked steel wheel of about 700 mm diameter[14];

ii) the load is positioned so that its weight acts just behind the line of the wheel axle. This minimises the portion of the load which must be supported by the operator, though he has to apply some upward force at the handles. This upward force facilitates control of the barrow when turning or traversing bumpy ground. The load is carried above or on either side of the wheel, often retained in light woven wicker baskets;

iii) the operator uses a strap which passes across his shoulders and is attached to the handles of the barrow. This overcomes the tendency of the barrow to tip sideways due to the placement of the load. To avoid possible discomfort the operator may wear a broad leather collar on which the strap rests.

Because of the location of the load and the low rolling resistance of the large wheel a greater weight can be carried on the Chinese wheelbarrow than is possible on the conventional type. These barrows are extensively used in China for earth-moving work on construction sites, frequently operating in large fleets with additional labour to provide assisted haulage on gradients. The evidence of Chinese literature is that the operation of these fleets is not haphazard but is carefully planned and organised[15].

Experience of the device outside China is still very limited. The World Bank have carried out tests on conventional and Chinese wheelbarrows. The large diameter (626 mm) of the motor-cycle wheel used on the Chinese wheelbarrow significantly reduced rolling resistance and increased operator comfort by eliminating jolting. Greater loads of up to 180 kg could be carried at speeds comparable with other barrows, but the use of the shoulder strap was essential. The hill-climbing ability of the Chinese wheelbarrow was good at shallow gradients, where the effect of the low rolling resistance was probably significant, but on steeper slopes it was worse than other configurations because of the greater load. Assisted hauling was tried as was winching, but it proved difficult to balance the barrow on very steep grades. The general conclusion of this initial study was that the advantages of the Chinese wheelbarrows became more apparent on the longer, flatter haulage runs in excess of about 50 m.

The available evidence strongly suggests that there is an important role for the Chinese wheelbarrow in labour-based civil construction. It is worthwhile to examine the technical effort still required to optimise its use.

Further study is needed in the following areas:
  i) determination of optimum wheel size, tyre width and tyre type, to minimise rolling resistance on the terrain found on construction sites;
  ii) development of designs for strong, light, large diameter wheels that can be manufactured in developing countries, using local resources where at all possible. Suitable wheels are not readily available in many places, and while those from motor cycles can be used they are expensive and not necessarily the optimum size;

iii) optimisation of the design of shoulder straps. For construction work it may be that the best solution is a harness worn by the operator, into which the barrow handles fit;
iv) investigation of the effect of the position of the load on the barrow, including its placement above the wheel, on either side of it, or some combination of the two, so as to determine the optimum weight distribution;
v) detailed examination of the techniques used in China; of particular interest would be the programming of labour for hauling, loading and assisting on steep slopes;
vi) extensive testing in different countries to gain field experience.

*Rail systems*. Rail systems — manually, animal or machine powered — have always been of considerable importance in mining and tunnelling. The ILO's pioneering study, *Men who move mountains*[16], was probably the first of recent attempts at evaluating the general usefulness of manually operated rail systems in civil construction. More recently still the IBRD have conducted some studies, also in India[17]. The IBRD found that the ease and frequency of track laying were crucial factors affecting the viability of a rail system. Thus, unless they can be made light and easily portable, manual rail systems are likely to be most viable when large quantities of material have to be moved over a fixed route. This is not often the case with road works unless the terrain is severe or centralised borrow-pits and quarries have to be exploited. Clearly their use is also very sensitive to the ruling gradients of the site. The ILO found that the maximum slope that could be managed comfortably by a team of 4 pushers was 1 in 40 (2.5 per cent) with a payload of 1,250 kg.

Both studies concluded that under the right conditions manually operated rail systems were capable of giving worker outputs at least 3 times as great as those using traditional methods. Notwithstanding this encouraging result, it has to be pointed out that in neither case could the quality of the experimental work be considered high. The equipment tested was largely "as found" with only minor development modifications. (The photographic evidence suggests that the trucks were designed for locomotive rather than manual haulage and thus were probably unnecessarily heavy.)

Clearly there is considerable scope for further development work on the vehicles and track which the ILO study both acknowledged and provided constructive suggestions for. These included[18]:
- determining the optimum capacity of the trucks;
- lowering the loading edge;
- improved shape to assist unloading;
- reduced weight;
- improved tipping geometry;
- provision of pushing bars; and
- improved winching arrangements where necessary.

It is worth nothing that manually powered rail systems are used in East Africa for harvesting sisal. The plantations are usually large and presumably the method is viable only because both the track and vehicles are light and have been designed for maximum portability.

*Pedal power.* The bicycle is ubiquitous throughout the developing world and in several countries — predominantly Asian — the pedal powered system of propulsion has been applied to goods carrying tricycles and, to a more limited extent, to stationary applications such as water pumping and crop processing. Although the principle of generating human power by applying the legs to rotating cranks is a highly effective and well-proven method[19], it does not seem to have been employed in civil construction[20].

Wilson[21] has pointed out that in terms of ergonomic efficiency (energy consumption per unit weight per unit distance) transport by cycle is supreme among moving creatures and machines. However, the cycles that have been developed for goods transport are invariably economically inefficient. Any form of gearing is rare so that acceleration from rest when loaded or ascending even modest gradients is very strenuous. Few have an efficient brake system and most are unnecessarily heavy, but these difficulties are relatively easy to overcome as Wilson[22] has shown. A recent study in Bangladesh emphasised the problems of the conversion of urban cycle rickshaws for use in the rural areas[23].

However, it is likely that the greatest potential for increasing the efficiency of human labour in civil construction by the use of pedal power lies in devices rather different from those employed in road transport. Such devices would be designed to meet the particular operational requirements of earthmoving activities. For example, a pedal-driven vehicle specifically designed for earthmoving might well be operated by more than one person, as in the radical concept proposed by Wilson[24]. Termed the "pedal rover" it is a four-wheel-drive vehicle having four large wheels, 1 or 1.1 m in diameter, each directly pedalled by one man sitting astride as on the early "penny-farthing" bicycles. The front and rear halves of the vehicle are hinged together at the centre in such a way as to provide steering (by means of cables) and also to allow relative twisting of the two halves to accommodate uneven ground without strain on the chassis. Since the weight of each rider is directly above each wheel and the load compartment is in line with the axles the bending load on the structure is minimised so a usefully large load, e.g. 400 kg should be possible with a modest vehicle weight.

Another possible application of pedal power to wheeled haulage is in the propulsion of rail carts, an innovation that could well enhance the productivity of these systems.

Finally, the available evidence[25] suggests that the useful power output of winches would be at least doubled by using a pedal drive system in place of hand-cranking. These could be applied to various aspects of construction such as hauling wheelbarrows up inclines.

## 4. Animal

The experimental work of ILO and IBRD shows that, under the right circumstances, animals can be a most appropriate source of power for haulage in civil construction. Yet, except in a few areas, they are rarely used for this work. In such continents as Africa, where the domestication of animals for work purposes is still uncommon this is understandable. However, the repudiation of animal-based agriculture as a backward step in the "modernisation" of African farming is becoming less common and the majority of countries are actively promoting its use. Thus, conditions are becoming more favourable for the use of animals in construction. In Asia, where animals are used extensively as a source of power, both in agriculture and in transport, their limited use in civil construction appears to result largely from the unsuitability of the indigenous technology, i.e. poor pannier and cart design.

*Animal panniers.* The use of animals equipped with panniers for hauling road construction materials is a very specialised technology that appears to be uncommon outside of certain parts of the Indian subcontinent. It is, however, a form of haulage that has peculiar advantages wherever the terrain results in uneven or steeply sloped working conditions and wheeled transport becomes inoperable. In these circumstances the famous surefootedness of the donkey and mule, in particular, come into their own. Experience in India[26] suggests that donkeys are capable of carrying 100-200 kg of earth (for haul lengths which typically are between 75 and 200 metres) in woven-rope panniers, but whether this is the maximum payload or optimum carrying device is uncertain[27]. In other countries horses and camels are used as pack animals, but little information is available on typical loads or the optimum design of panniers for the carriage of soil. Indeed a recent IBRD literature survey[28] found very little information which was directly relevant to the use of animals in civil construction and nothing to suggest that any substantial research had been done in this field.

Clearly there is considerable scope for improving our understanding of the use of pack animals in construction activities. The major area for improvement is pannier design which is likely to affect not only the maximum load that can be carried but perhaps more important, the speed with which it can be loaded and unloaded.

*Animal carts.* In the countries where animal carts are common there is a growing appreciation that the scope for improving their general design is considerable. India, perhaps the home of the bullock cart, is actively trying to overcome the defects of designs that have hardly changed since the Mohanjadaro civilisation (3000 — 2000 BC). Pioneering work in identifying these defects has been done by Mr. N.S. Ramaswamy, Director of the Indian Institute of Management (IIM), Bangalore[29]. The major drawbacks of the traditional vehicles are poor axle bearings, wobbling wheels, excessive tare weight, the absence of a braking device, excessive friction between the road and the wheel, and poor weight distribution over the cart length. But the worst part of the design is the damage and cruelty caused to the animals. A crude harnessing device, a wooden bar, rests on the animal's neck in front of the hump, making the skin calloused and very often cancerous. Moreover, in the traditional design, the animal's neck forms one of the resting points of the payload. Almost invariably these factors are wasteful of pulling power since they conspire to exert a throttling force on the animal in proportion to the effort it attempts to exert: it is hardly surprising that the animals appear unwilling to work!

In conditions encountered on construction sites, a pneumatic tyred wheel running on ball bearings is likely to be more appropriate than traditional wooden designs, and the intensive use of the carts should justify the higher cost involved. Pneumatic tyres specifically intended for animal cart use are manufactured commercially in India under the name ADV (Animal Drawn Vehicle). A simple way of constructing a cart with this type of wheel is to use an old truck axle complete with hub mountings. However, this is likely to be excessively heavy, and a better approach is to develop a fabricated axle. In a joint project, the IIM and College of Engineering, Coimbator have designed a new cart for rural use which has a lightweight integrated chassis and draw-bar fixed on a fabricated axle. This is said to cost little more than the traditional design.

The problems of traditional yoke harnesses can probably best be overcome by the use of the three-pad collar harness developed in Germany some 40 years ago, and now used universally on European bullock carts[30]. This harness rests on pads on the neck and shoulders while leaving the front of the neck unrestricted so that the animal can breathe freely. In addition to eliminating the discomfort of the animal the harness transmits its power, which is generated largely by the strong shoulder muscles, more effectively. It has been estimated that this harness can double the useful output of the animal[31].

It is necessary to recognise that materials haulage for civil construction poses its own peculiar requirements for cart design: low loading height and ease of unloading. Neither problem has received much attention, but there are signs that this is changing. In the Philippines the ILO[32] modified the traditional animal-drawn cart by substituting a removable bamboo mat for the fixed floor, thus enabling a crude form of "bottom discharge" to be effected.

There have also been various attempts to produce a cart

whose body can be tipped without unyoking the animals for the unloading operation, notably at the Agricultural Farm, Nagpur, in India[33] and at Ahmadu Bello University in Nigeria[34].

All single-axle carts must invariably cause much stress to the animals, with consequent loss of pulling power, under the rough surface conditions typical of construction sites. Therefore, a more beneficial line of development might be with two-axled carts. These were the dominant means of haulage during the great era of European railway and canal construction. In many cases a light rail track was laid and the cart equipped with flanged railway-type wheels. This is arguably a *forgotten* rather than an *inferior* technology since the labour productivities were typically six times as great as those currently achieved in labour-based earthwork operations in developing countries. Since the latter are already competitive with equipment-based methods in some circumstances, the potential benefits of raising labour productivities towards the levels achieved in the past are considerable. The available evidence suggests that the operation of animal-drawn carts on light construction rails is a technology that is worthy of re-examination.

*Animal-drawn scrapers*. The main application of these devices is for the movement over short distances of previously loosened earth.

Although this is not included in the list of methods given in table 1, they have been used in the past, particularly for the levelling of land for agricultural purposes. More recently the ILO has demonstrated their suitability for road construction during studies in the Philippines[35]. The report on these studies makes clear that there is scope for improving the design and manufacture of the scrapers which were developed from the traditional bamboo (originally Chinese) scraper used in agriculture. Furthermore it seems likely from the photographic evidence of the experiments that the harnessing arrangements could also be improved in the same way as for bullock carts. The range of soils for which scrapers can be used will be proportional to the tractive effort the animal(s) can provide and this is very sensitive to the harnessing system.

## 5. Engines

There exists at present a huge gulf in terms of power output between animal-drawn earthmoving devices and conventional capital plant such as scrapers, dozers and dump trucks. It is therefore, worthwhile to consider the potential, in earthmoving for using devices powered by small, low-output engines. In general, diesel engines are likely to be more suitable for construction work than petrol engines for reasons of reliability, longevity, maintenance and running costs.

*Single-axle tractor.* The two-wheeled, or as it is more commonly known, single-axle tractor, powered by a single cyclinder 7.5-9 kw (10-12 hp) diesel engine has played a vital role in the mechanisation of Chinese agriculture and is also a major element of the rural transport system when hitched to a trailer[36]. In this mode it provides transport from the commune to the town and back again, with a payload of 1,000 kg and a maximum speed of 15 km/hr. It would appear from the evidence that single-axle tractors are also used for some construction activities in China, but the extent of this practice is not known.

Single-axle tractors are now beginning to find a place in India, and in the Philippines where some 7,000 machines are produced each year to a design developed at the International Rice Research Institute (IRRI)[37]. The IRRI design, which sells for about half the price of comparable imports, is illustrative of how such a device can be produced economically by small industries in developing countries. IRRI have achieved this by developing a design which makes extensive use of readily available components such as motor-cycle and automotive parts, and limits production operations to fabrication and simple machining. Single-axle tractors are also used on a wide scale in agriculture in Switzerland,' Germany and Austria.

Single-axle tractors could be used in civil construction for hauling and for other operations (e.g. ploughing, ripping, grubbing, rotavating, etc.) since they have much of the flexibility associated with conventional, but very much more expensive, agricultural tractors. Their principal advantages would appear to be low-cost and robust simplicity, but whether these qualities are cost effective when employed as an aid to labour on civil construction remains unproven.

*Small cargo carriers.* A wide range of three-wheeled, motor-cycle based vehicles are used in cities in Asia, Southern Europe and Central America for goods and passenger transport. In certain places the operation of these vehicles has begun to extend from urban to rural areas. Partly as a result of this, and also because of the influence of single-axle tractors, a new breed of three-wheelers is emerging specifically designed to meet the more arduous conditions and somewhat different requirements of rural transport. Perhaps the most notable are a number of cargo carriers now being manufactured on the island of Crete[38]. These differ in details of design, but typically use a single-cylinder diesel engine of 6-9 kw (8-12 hp), have a payload of about 1,000 kg and maximum speed of 40-45 km/hr. These vehicles are robust, easy to maintain, and can be produced economically by small-scale enterprises. In the Philippines the IRRI has developed a motorised cart consisting of a single motorised and steered wheel hitched to the front of a two-wheeled trailer. This was originally designed as a means of transporting a portable rice thresher from place to place, but is now in great demand as a general-purpose goods carrier[39].

With the exception of a water bowser similar vehicles for civil construction have not been evolved, yet there would seem to be considerable potential for their use. Light, fast and maneouvrable yet robust vehicles based on a well-established technology should logically be intermediate in application between the simplicity of animal power on the one hand and the complexity and *expense* of conventional tractors or capital earthmoving plant on the other. There is some evidence that this is being recognised. They are especially favoured by municipal maintenance organisations whose activities typically involve restricted loads and journey lengths for which their use is economic. Serious attempts to extend the use of such vehicles to civil construction and to determine what potential, if any, they possess, have yet to be undertaken.

*Tractor-trailers*. Theoretically the tractor-trailer combination appears very attractive for labour-based construction. It is usually presumed that in agricultural communities tractors should be available for at least part of the year. However, the main justification for considering them as complementary to labour-based construction is that one tractor can be used with several trailers for transporting spoil of fill material. Thus, instead of a whole dump-truck unit standing idle whilst it is being hand loaded, only the trailer is stationary: the tractor, which is the expensive component of the combination, is fully occupied in shuttling trailers back and forth. It also has several other useful capabilities such as ground preparation by ploughing and ripping; grubbing; rotavating for mix-in-place lime, cement or bitumen stabilisation; compaction with towed rollers; and general haulage of water, cement, culverts, labour etc. The IBRD has published comprehensive advice on the use of tractor-trailer combinations in civil construction together with analytical methods for assessing their viability in relation to conventional trucks[40]. However, practical experience of their use is very limited. The most ambitious attempt to use them in road construction has been in the Kenya Rural Access Roads Programme[41]. This has given valuable experience on the most appropriate forms of tractor-trailer combination. It has also shown that trailers, in particular, need to be very carefully constructed if they are to withstand the rigours of a construction site and special designs have had to be produced[42].

A further lesson from the Kenya experience relates to tractor size. Initially, 75 hp tractors were specified, but smaller, 45 hp machines have now been substituted. These smaller tractors are considerably cheaper, are quite satisfactory for the work involved and, since they haul smaller trailers with reduced sill height, loading by shovel is easier[43].

## 6. Discussion

We have sought to demonstrate that there is considerable scope both to *improve*, and to introduce *innovations* into the range of equipment currently used for labour-based road construction. We have done so by considering only the "earthmoving" phase, but the arguments and conclusions could be applied equally to the other phases of civil construction. The purpose of either improvements or innovations would be to increase the competitiveness of labour with machinery and thereby its employment prospects. However, it would be mistaken to think that the technical problems are so simple that they can be solved with little effort or skill. Experience has shown that it often requires the very best technological skills to solve, what look to the untrained eye, to be simple problems. The humble wheelbarrow has been used in civil construction for well over 100 years yet the great majority continue to be badly engineered and, in a scientific sense, to contain fundamental deficiencies in design. Neither of these problems will be overcome without the best technological skills.

To suggest that an alternative technological choice exists or that traditional techniques can be upgraded is, of course, merely the first step. There are considerable obstacles both to their development and application.

The manufacturers of capital equipment are very organised nationally and internationally, and well able to promote their products among government agencies and to supply adequate maintenance and spare parts facilities. There are no comparable pressure groups of manufacturers for equipment suitable for labour-based construction and because there are few present demands, maintenance and spares are poor or non-existent. Indeed, for most of the equipment described in this chapter there is rarely any indication of whether local manufacturers would be capable of meeting demands if they existed. Conversely without such a demand an entrepreneur is unlikely to invest in producing, say, an improved animal-drawn scraper unless he is reasonably sure that sales will at least cover costs. Under these circumstances credit to finance such an investment is also equally doubtful. To overcome these obstacles will require an initial financial commitment by government to develop and test the type of equipment described. If this is successful then the equipment could be used on various pilot projects to establish its long-term efficiency.

It is important that the development engineers should work in co-operation with potential local manufacturers preferably in the small-scale sector to ensure that the equipment is sutiable for indigenous production. At the production stage it may well be necessary to assist local manufacturers with finance, with technical advice and with support in such matters as ensuring the supply of specified materials in the small quantities which are all their limited capital resources will permit. However, perhaps the most important form of assistance, if small industries are to accept the risk involved in embarking on a new manufacturing venture, is to ensure that they have a secure market for their products.

Certain of the technologies which are described in this chapter already exist in some countries but have not been applied in others, or have not been used in labour-based road construction. If the maximum benefit is to be realised from these, and from hardware development programmes in different parts of the world, then there is a need to make detailed information on new or improved implements widely available.

As has been shown, the potential for improving the technology of labour-based road construction is virtually untapped, and there is no shortage of soundly based ideas to be developed and tested. What is needed now is the will and commitment to do so.

**Notes and references**

[1] Secretariat of the Economic and Social Commission for Asia and the Pacific. *Manual labour and its more effective use in competition with machines for earthwork in the ECAFE region*, Paper of the Proceedings of the Third Regional Technical Conference on Water Resources Development in Asia and the Far East, The United Nations Flood Control Series Publication No. 13, Bangkok (1958)

[2] See Chapter 5.

[3] After P.A. Green and P.D. Brown, *Some aspects of the use of labour-intensive methods for road construction*, Indian Roads Congress, 37th Annual Session (New Delhi), November 1976.

[4] *Study of the substitution of labour and equipment in civil construction. Tech. Memo. 12: Haulage by headbasket, shoulder yokes and other manual load-carrying methods.* (IBRD, October 1975).

[5] *Men who move mountains: an account of a research project with manual methods of earthmoving.* (ILO, Geneva, 1963)

[6] ILO, *Men who move mountains*, op. cit.

[7] *Study of the substitution of labour and equipment in civil construction. Tech. Memo. 1: Comparison of alternative design wheelbarrows for use in civil construction tasks* (IBRD, January 1975).

[8] *Study of the substitution of labour and equipment in civil construction. Tech. Memo. 3: Comparison of different modes of haulage in earthworks* (IBRD, June 1975).

[9] *Study of the substitution of labour and equipment in civil construction. Tech. Memo. 13: The use of wheelbarrows in civil construction* (IBRD, October 1975)

[10] T. Coleman, *The railway navvies* (London, Penguin Books, 1976).

[11] J. Needham, *Science and civilisation in China*, Vol. 4, Part 2 (London, Cambridge University Press, 1971).

¹² S.S. Wilson, "The Wheelbarrow" *Appropriate Technology*, May 1975.
¹³ R.P. Hommel, *China at work* (London, M.I.T. Press, 1969).
¹⁴ I.J. Barwell, "Chinese handcarts and wheelbarrows", *Appropriate Technology*, August 1976.
¹⁵ Anon, *Harm into benefit* (Peking, Foreign Language Press, 1975).
¹⁶ *Men who move mountains*, op. cit.
¹⁷ *Study of the substitution of labour and equipment in civil construction. Tech. Memo.23: The use of rail systems in civil construction* (IBRD, June 1976)
¹⁸ ILO, *Men who move mountains*, op. cit., p. 219.
¹⁹ F.R. Whitt and D.G. Wilson, *Bicycling science: ergonomics and mechanics* (M.I.T. Press, Cambridge (Mass) and London, 1974).
²⁰ The Chinese are known to have developed pedal-driven belt conveyors for earthmoving, also pedal-driven bucket conveyors and a floating pedal-driven scoop dredger, but few details are available.
²¹ S.S. Wilson, "Bicycle technology", *Scientific American*, March 1973.
²² S.S. Wilson, "Pedal power on land: the Third World and beyond", Chapter 2 in *Pedal Powder* (Rodale Press, 1977).
²³ I.J. Barwell, "Review of appropriate technologies for road transport in Bangladesh," ITDG, March 1978.
²⁴ "Pedal power on land: the Third World and beyond", op. cit.
²⁵ "Pedal power on land: the Third World and beyond", op. cit.
²⁶ IBRD Tech. Memo.3, *op. cit.*
²⁷ Information from Pakistan gives figures of 90-150 kg for haul distances up to 400 metres: *Study of the use of labour-intensive methods for the Indus super highway in Pakistan* (ILO, Geneva, 1977).
²⁸ *Study of the substitution of labour and equipment in civil construction. Tech. Memo.21: A literature review of the work output of animals with particular reference to their use in civil construction* (IBRD, February 1976).
²⁹ N.S. Ramaswamy, "Reducing animal power wastage and mitigating cruelty to work animals", *Indian Institute of Management Occasional Papers, Vol. 1, No. 8*, Bangalore, 1977.
³⁰ H.J. Hopfen, *Farm implements for arid and tropical regions* (FAO, Rome, 1969).
³¹ Y. Orev, "Improved farming system for Botswana", *Appropriate Technology*, Vol. 4, No 2, August 1977.
³² Deepak Lal, et al., *Men or machines?* (ILO, Geneva 1978).
³³ "India works on the twentieth century bullock cart", *New Scientist*, 13 January, 1977.

[34] R.M. Schneider, *The Samaru ox cart*, Samaru Miscellaneous Paper No. 20, Institute for Agricultural Research, Ahmadu Bello University, Zaria, Nigeria, 1967.

[35] ILO, *Men or machines* op. cit.

[36] I.J. Barwell, Chinese two-wheeled tractor, *World crops and livestock*, July/August 1977.

[37] A.U. Khan, *Mechanisation technology for tropical agriculture*, OECD Study Group on Low-Cost Technology and Rural Industrialisation, Paris, 1974.

[38] A.K. Meier, *Three-wheeled vehicles in Crete*, Lawrence Berkeley Laboratory, University of California, 1977 (mimeographed).

[39] IRRI, *Rice machinery development and mechanisation research*, Agricultural Engineering Department Semi-Annual Progress Report, July-December 1975.

[40] *Study of the substitution of labour and equipment in civil construction. Tech. Memo.24: The use of agricultural tractor/trailer combinations (IBRD, February 1976).*

[41] *Implementation of appropriate road construction technology in Kenya*, report of the joint Ministry of Works/ILO/NORAD project (ILO, Geneva, November 1976).

[42] W. Armstrong, *Kenya rural access roads programme: Hand tools and equipment improvement, procurement, marketing*. Small Industry Report No. 1, Ministry of Overseas Development, London 1976.

[43] *Kenya rural access roads programme: Hand tools and equipment improvement, procurement, marketing*, op. cit.

# CHAPTER 5. THE PRIVATE CONSTRUCTION SECTOR AND APPROPRIATE TECHNOLOGY

*by A.D. Austen*

## 1. Introduction

The three previous chapters have been concerned with problems of implementation. By and large they have viewed the issue from the standpoint of the government. In this chapter we look at the private sector and the implications for it in the use of appropriate technology. For most developing countries, the provision of roads, houses, irrigation, water supply and sanitation accounts for a major portion of annual capital expenditure. Furthermore, industrial development, too, has a large construction element. Thus, whatever the political, social or economic theories may be which determine the allocation of national resources, the translation of development plans into reality relies heavily on the construction sector. It is also true to say that, without exception, the implementation of government programmes of infrastructure development is in the hands of government ministries, departments or state enterprises. Inevitably, such programmes involve an ever-increasing expenditure on the maintenance of the works which they produce.

Despite the fact that the money for infrastructure development, and indeed for a great deal of industrial development, comes from government and that government agencies are almost exclusively responsible for implementation, the private construction sector plays a major part in the execution of these programmes in most of the countries of Asia and the Pacific. It is therefore not sufficient to consider the problems and implications of appropriate technology as they affect government agencies only, we must also take into account the instrument by which those agencies execute many of their schemes — in other words, the private construction sector.

In order to do this, it is necessary to examine the nature of the industry which has unique characteristics. Many millions of words have been written on this subject, so in this paper attention is concentrated on those factors which influence the neglect, adoption or rejection of appropriate technology in the private sector. This is done by first of all discussing the environment within which the industry operates, and then considering the latter's internal structure. Finally, some suggestions are made as to how some of the factors which inhibit the application of appropriate technology may be removed.

It is of course realised that in a regional context both the analysis of problems and suggestions for their solution is necessarily generalised, since conditions vary from country to country. Nevertheless, there is likely to be sufficient similarity in the nature of the problems encountered to engender a meaningful discussion, although ultimately each country must evolve its own national solutions for its national problems.

## 2. The operating environment of the construction industry

The market for the products of the industry is dominated by the government. This is probably a universal fact, but because of the greater need for infrastructure development in developing countries, the dominance amounts to a near monopoly. Therefore, government policies, legislation, regulations and the attitudes of its civil servants are largely responsible for moulding the industry into its present form. This does not imply inevitability, exclude the possibility of change, or remove all responsibility from the shoulders of the private sector but, as in nature, the contractor must adapt to his environment or perish.

Another important factor is the existence in many countries of a large pool of unemployed and underemployed workers who can be hired and fired on a casual basis. Indeed, it has been stated[1] that, in India at least, this is the major reason for the lack of innovation within the industry.

This operating environment is now discussed under the following headings:
- government policies;
- conditions of contract;

- attitudes;
- functional divisions;
- employment.

## 2.1 *Government policies*

The construction sector is used by many countries, both industrialised and developing, as a crude but effective economic regulator. When the chill winds of recession blow it is a relatively simple matter to slow down or stop the construction of motorways, power stations, water supplies, houses, etc., since all of these depend on government financing. That many thousands are thereby thrown out of work is unfortunate, but politically is not too disastrous since the construction industry even in a highly industrialised country relies heavily on casual labour. Such labour is accustomed to cyclical swings, and also tends to be less organised than labour in other industries. Furthermore, the impact on the ultimate consumer is not immediate, since most construction projects are relatively long term, so that by the time the effect of the non-provision of a motorway or the reduction in maintenance is felt by the general public the economy may again be on the upswing, in which case public protest will be muted. A current example of the converse situation is to be seen in Japan where, in order to stimulate domestic demand, the Government has embarked on an ambitious public works programme.

Thus, whether used as a brake or an accelerator, construction offers a simple and politically safe way of controlling the economy, and its appeal is therefore irresistible, although there are many cogent agruments why such a policy is a short-sighted one.

It is not only at the macro level that government policies affect the industry, but also at the micro level. In most Asian countries, construction budgets are allocated annually by the treasury or budget bureau. This means that even projects which have started may find themselves without funds when the annual budget is allocated, since short-term financial considerations rather than longer-term economic objectives or engineering logic reign supreme.

In many countries, construction is not recognised as an industry in the same way as are manufacturing or processing or steel making or mining, etc. This means there is no legislation framed specifically for construction. However, it does have to operate within, for example, a factories act. This can produce some very strange results: if the factory act requires that the air in the factory be kept free of dust, and a worksite is a factory within the meaning of the act, then a 10, 50 or 100-mile road construction project is a site, and how do you keep *that* free of dust? In practical terms, of course, everybody realises that in these circumstances the law is just not applicable, but this means that the law falls into disrepute, and then such important matters as the safety, health and welfare of workers in the industry are not adequately provided for.

For the private contractor, this lack of recognition means that not only does he lack the status of other industrialists but that he probably has problems in raising capital from lending institutions. These problems are particularly acute for the smaller contractor and are intensified if he is using a labour-based technology, since this means that his fixed assets of equipment and plant are lower in relation to his working capital than in a machine-based technology. Even if lending institution can be persuaded to lend money to this category of contractor, it will only be against the security of his fixed assets and not to meet his weekly or monthly wage bill, so that the larger the latter is relative to the former the more difficulties he faces, particularly as contract payments will usually be at least one month behind work completion.

## 2.2 *Conditions of contract and government regulations*

It is the usual practice that contractors working for the government are classified according to its own assessment of their capacity to carry out projects up to certain maximum values. The criteria used for the assessment will include such factors as financial standing, technical staff, experience, and available plant. The greater the value of the contracts to be undertaken, the more need there is assumed to be for larger items of mechanical equipment. This could mean that the small contractor proposing to use bullock-drawn carts and scrapers would not get on the register of approved contractors because, for example, there was a requirement that he own at least two tipper lorries and a grader, whilst a larger contractor prepared to mobilise a large labour force using appropriate technology equipment would also not qualify as a major contractor because he was required to own heavy earthmoving equipment.

In addition to regulations governing the contractor in his tendering for government contracts, the conditions of contract and specification themselves often militate against the use of appropriate technology. These are in general based on western practices and may therefore specify the use of plant when there may be alternative methods of achieving the same result. Performance specifications are still relatively rare — that is to say, a specification stating what the performance of the finished product should be without stating how that performance should be achieved. Thus, a base course might be required to have a dry density of 100 per cent, without going on to say that it will be given a minimum number of passes of a 12-ton roller. Of course, the use of this type of specification implies technical competence on the part of the contractor, and particularly in the case of small contractors this is frequently lacking. Nevertheless, the specifications presently in use do inhibit the use of any new or different technology.

## 2.3 *Attitudes*

As soon as one begins to discuss attitudes, one is moving into a somewhat subjective and sensitive area. Nevertheless, since attitudes do have an important bearing on the subject of application of appropriate technology, they should be discussed openly and frankly.

The attitude of the professional engineer to the private contractor will naturally vary from person to person and will be coloured by all sorts of complex relationships, but certain behavioural patterns can be detected. Among these is a feeling of superiority arising from superior technical knowledge, superior education, and something of a master-servant relationship. Do not think that this is unique to the Asian scene — even today in industrialised countries the term "contractor" often has a denigratory connotation, but this is far less the case than it used to be.

Coupled with this feeling of superiority is a tinge of envy, since the contractor may be making a great deal more money than the professional engineer, many of whom are relatively poorly paid. Thus, the large Mercedes, the unlimited expense account, the modern house are conspicuous marks of success to which the engineer cannot attain.

Finally, there may be a feeling of guilt and dependence if the engineer is engaged in corrupt practices. This is naturally a very sensitive area, but it is no use pretending that these things do not occur, and none of our societies, whether of the East or West, is free of such practices, which have a marked effect on the relationships between engineers and contractors.

Now an industrial psychologist could undoubtedly explain these relationships in technical terms and the above may appear rather simplistic; what matters, however, is the effect on the application of appropriate technology. The principal effect is that because contracting is regarded as somewhat inferior to engineering, there is reluctance on the part of qualified engineers to move over into the private sector. This is much more marked in the case of the small contractor, since the large contractor can offer status and compensatory awards for the engineer who moves over. The net result is that the small private contractors are starved of the talent which could introduce new ideas and improved technologies. It may be argued that there is no reason why the engineer should not be able to infuse these ideas into the private sector from his existing position, but he is not motivated to do so. The engineer accepts no responsibility for the actual execution of the work and would regard any effort on his part to introduce new ideas as merely contributing to increased profits on the part of the contractor without any benefit to himself.

These attitudes, then, mean that the private contractor is nearly always regarded as innately inferior in status to the engineer, and this is self-perpetuating since it starves him of the managerial and technical expertise which he needs to improve his status. It is this talent which could make him more innovative and thus more likely to adopt appropriate technologies.

### 2.4 *Functional divisions*

Much has been written about the inefficiencies arising from a system whereby the responsibilities for design and for construction are usually separate and distinct, so it is not intended to rehearse the arguments. What this does mean is that there is no incentive whatsoever for the contractor to innovate. He is given a design, he is expected to stick strictly to that design and, incidentally, he is still held to be responsible if the structure falls down. Furthermore, the contractor is in business, naturally enough, to make a profit, and the only way he can be sure of doing this is by working within the system and relying on conventional methods. His instinctive reaction to the suggestion that he try something different will be: "Show me it working successfully and profitably somewhere else, then I might consider it".

Not only does the construction system militate against innovation, but it also offers no real incentive for efficiency, and this is especially true as regards small contractors. On the face of it, a system whereby every project is open to competitive bidding, and where the lowest tender must be accepted, should result in a high level of efficiency, but in practice this is not so, for the following reasons:

a) The contractor has no control over the design and specification of the product he manufactures. In this respect he differs radically from the man who manufactures teapots, for example. If the latter can improve his design and the efficiency of his manufacture he can presumably sell more teapots at a higher profit. The incentive therefore exists for him to do some market research to find out what his customers want, then to design a teapot which will not only satisfy market needs but which will be economic to produce. The system prevents anything similar happening in the construction sector, since the contractor can influence neither the design nor the market for his product. (Like all analogies this one must not be pushed too far, but it serves to illustrate the point.)

b) The competitive tendering system merely establishes a market price, it does not contribute one iota to efficiency. A contractor can still make an adequate profit even though he is operating inefficiently, provided that he is operating at about the same level as other contractors. For any given project, the material content is fixed so that the size of the contractor's margin depends on only two factors: (1) his overhead costs, and (2) his labour productivity. Now the overhead costs of the small contractor in particular are likely to be very low — he

probably works from an office in his house and has a staff of a foreman and a clerk-cum-storekeeper. There is therefore little or no scope for any reduction. This leaves labour productivity. All the small contractors working in a particular area will be drawing on the same pool of labour, and that labour will employ the traditional tools and methods, so that productivity will not vary greatly whether the labour works for contractor A, B or C. Furthermore, the contractor's profit margin will not be affected because all the contractors are adding a percentage to what might be called the lowest common denominator of labour output.
c) Finally, the engineer's estimate of the final product, be it a road or an irrigation system or a building, is almost always known before tenders are invited. This estimate is necessary for budgeting purposes, and most engineers tend to be conservative when preparing it since over-expenditure on a project will involve them in interminable arguments with their financial controllers. It therefore establishes a maximum figure beyond which any bid is almost certain to be rejected. On the other hand, it certainly does not necessarily represent an estimate of a reasonable price, assuming efficient operation on the part of the contractor. Experience soon teaches a contractor what percentage below this figure he must bid at to have a reasonable chance of winning.

Thus, the way in which the total cnstruction system is organised, and about which the contractor can do nothing, is inefficient, and the spur of real competition is lacking. Safe and traditional methods of working are therefore preferred and the adoption of appropriate technology is inhibited.

## 2.5 *Employment*

One of the unique characteristics of construction which has an important bearing on the industry's attitude towards innovation is the structure of the labour force. Not only is the proportion of unskilled labour very high, but this labcur is employed on a casual basis. Most of the reasons for this are well known:
- lack of continuity in work supply to the contractor;
- the "one-off" nature of the projects;

- climatic conditions;
- the wish on the part of employers to avoid social welfare obligations.

The most important reason, however, is the existence in most if not all of the countries in Asia of a large pool of labour which is willing, nay anxious, to work on this basis.

Thus, the employer, whether government or private, can easily match his fluctuating workload with a fluctuating workforce. Add to this that the workforce is unorganised, illiterate and poor, that the contractor can still make a reasonable profit margin despite the low productivity of his workers, and one sees why the industry has no incentive to change. As Johri and Pandey[2] say, "...the industry is capable of quantitative expansion but not of qualitative change". This is especially true of the small contractor who often works with a technology which has not changed for centuries.

Given then that the industry has no incentive to adopt an improved technology largely because of the existence of a large pool of unskilled labour, the dilemma that must be faced is: if by some means it *were* persuaded to adopt an appropriate technology, would not the improvement in productivity result in the employment of *fewer* workers?

Let us look at this a little more closely.

It is of course true that if productivity can be increased, then for a given total output the labour input will decrease. If these inputs and outputs are expressed in money terms, this means that the difference between the two will also increase.

There are then three ways in which this differential can be used:

a) improved wages for the workers;
b) higher profits for the contractor;
c) lower total cost for the client (usually the government).

The first of these is obviously of benefit to the worker and achieves one of the objectives of the ILO's World Employment Programme — that is better income distribution — whilst the third benefits the community as a whole. It has already been pointed out that the contractor can make a reasonable profit margin despite low productivity, and this is an argument for not giving him higher profits; on the other hand, since we want to encourage him to increase productivity, some incentive is probably necessary. The way in which the benefits arising from improved productivity are distributed is an example of a situation where one cannot pontificate on a regional basis; each country must decide for itself in the light of its national circumstances. What is generally certain is that if the application of appropriate technology results in increased productivity the industry has the opportunity to break out of the vicious circle of primitive technology leading to low productivity leading to low wages leading back to primitive technology because we cannot afford to pay higher wages.

This still leaves unsolved, however, the problem of increasing the total amount of employment available, even though the wages and conditions of those who *are* employed can be improved. The clue here lies in the use of word "substitution". Thus the World Bank calls its study "the substitution of labour (sic) and equipment in civil construction"[3]. The implication is clear, namely that work which would otherwise be done by machine can become available for labour, subject of course to the various constraints that have been discussed. Thus the reduction in total employment arising from increased productivity can be more than compensated for by increasing the market share of labour-intensive projects. Indeed, it is a prerequisite of increasing the share of the market that productivity be increased so as to compete with capital-intensive technologies. Furthermore, a private sector equipped with appropriate tools and techniques will possess the enterprise to seize the opportunities thus presented.

In summary, the existence of a large pool of unskilled labour enables the private contractor, especially the small one, to expand and contract to suit the market without any need for internal change. His margins are unaffected by low productivity, there is little genuine competition, so the impetus for innovation is negligible. If, however, the right environment and motivation can be found for the application of appropriate technology, productivity will increase, wages and conditions of workers will improve and the greater share of the market now available will result in employment creation.

## 3. Structure of the private construction sector

This is characterised by two extremes: the large contractor, indistinguishable in most respects from his counterpart in the industrialised world, and the very small local contractor short of capital, equipment and know-how. This represents an important difference from the situation in the industrialised countries where, in addition to these extremes, there is a middle section comprising medium-scale contractors, many of whom are old established and competent within the limitations of their capacity. The existence of a more or less complete spectrum means that movement across it is a possibility for those that wish to make it, whereas, in Asia, to cross the gap would require a leap beyond the capability of most. Thus the small contractor remains trapped in a situation from which he cannot escape by his own efforts.

Let us examine a little more closely these two extremes; firstly, the large contractor.

## 3.1 *The large contractor*

In this category are included state-owned corporations, such as the National Engineering Corporation of Nepal, or the National Buildings Construction Corporation of India, since, although these are government owned, they are intended to operate in the same way as a private contractor, and they are generally similarly structured. Large can only be defined quantitatively in the context of each individual country, since what is large in Afghanistan with a population of 19.5 million[4] may be small in Indonesia with a population of 134.7 million, but in the sense of this paper a large contractor is one capable of undertaking major construction projects such as highways, major irrigation schemes, housing developments, hotel developments, etc., whilst a small contractor is one capable only of building rural roads, minor irrigation schemes, small housing projects, etc.

In the early stages of development of most countries in the Asian region, there was no local contracting industry capable of carrying out major works, many of which depended also on large amounts of foreign capital, so it was perhaps inevitable that foreign contractors should be brought in. In course of time, local businessmen seized the opportunities afforded by an expanding construction sector and set up as contractors, modelling themselves, naturally enough, on the examples before them and frequently starting as subcontractors. The more successful of these entered into joint ventures with the foreign companies, and in many cases ultimately took over all the business, although sometimes retaining a name linking them with the parent company. Examples of these are Ital-Thai in Thailand, and McDonald Layton Costain of Pakistan.

At this end of the spectrum, therefore, we have large contractors of three types:
- a) international contractors, usually working on large projects financed by IBRD or ADB;
- b) joint venture contractors working on similar projects, but some of which may be locally financed;
- c) local contractors (including state corporations) working on large national government and private contracts.

All three categories will, however, have similar financial and organisational structures, which is hardly surprising since, as indicated above, they are all descended from the same stock and they are all working within the same kind of contractual framework.

An important feature of the operation of the large local contractor is the extent to which the work is executed through subcontractors, and this has widespread implications, which will be examined later. These subcontractors are essentially suppliers of skilled labour only, and generally do not supply materials or equipment which remain the responsibility of the main contractor. This is not to imply that they are only agents for the supply of labour — they are more than that, since they undertake to carry out certain sections of the work for a fixed price or at an agreed rate. Thus the carpentry subcontractor will agree to fix the centring for a bridge span at a certain price, with the main contractor supplying the necessary timber, scaffolding, etc., but with the subcontractor supplying and paying all the labour, for which the main contractor accepts no responsibility. An important consequence of this is that this labour does not appear on the payroll of the main contractor. This constitutes an important difference between large national contractors in Asia and those in Europe since, although the latter frequently use subcontractors, the use of labour-only subcontractors is generally illegal.

This type of subcontractor constitutes an informal group within the formal organisation of the main contractor and will be bound together by traditional ties of craftsmanship, tribe, caste, religion, and so on. Operating as it does in a competitive market, and often with a high demand for its skills, this group, which resembles in some ways the old guilds of Europe, has a vested interest in restricting membership and is thus not very susceptible to change.

The implication of the foregoing as far as appropriate technology is concerned is that the large contractor is unlikely to be very interested. He operates in the tradition of his counterpart in the industrialised world, where the emphasis is on labour saving; the system of labour-only subcontracting removes from him most of the problems associated with the management of men rather than machines; the subcontractors themselves have a vested interest in maintaining their exclusiveness. In addition to the consequent reluctance on the part of the large contractor to adopt appropriate technology, the project design and specification requirements may provide a genuine reason why he cannot.

## 3.2 *The small contractor*

In the almost complete absence of statistics, and having regard to the great diversity of countries in the region, it is impossible to define quantitatively what is meant by a small contractor. It is, however, generally understood to mean one who is capable of small-scale works only, such as rural road construction and improvement, small-span bridges, culverts, and so forth. He may be a carpenter or mason possessed of the initiative to set up business on his own, although this is more likely to be the case in building than in road construction. Alternatively he may be an entrepreneur to whom contracting is merely one outlet for the capacity for seizing opportunities, taking risks, adapting and working hard, which characterise his kind. Whether he be one or the other, entry into or exit from the industry is remarkably easy. As the ILO study of labour-based road construction in Iran[5] says, " ... it is possible to build a road with no more than a telephone, so to speak, while holding one or more other jobs as well ... ". This type of contractor has no real commitment to the industry, and is not therefore particularly interested in the investment in human resources which is necessary if long-term improvements are to be achieved.

Not only this, but with limited capital resources it is easier to get credit for the hire of machines than for the payment of wages, added to which there is the problem of managing people, which is also more difficult than managing machines.

The situation described above relates specifically to Iran. In many countries in Asia there is no equipment-rental market, so that the question of the small contractor hiring machines does not arise. Unfortunately, he knows of no alternatives: either he uses primitive and unproductive methods or he needs sophisticated machines. This is precisely where appropriate technology fits into the picture by providing the appropriate mix of labour and machines to bridge the gap.

The constraints which trap the small contractor are:
- lack of capital and the difficulty of obtaining credit for payment of wages;
- lack of managerial know-how;
- lack of technical expertise;
- too great a gap between the large western-style contractor and himself.

Above all, as discussed under the heading "Employment", there is the lack of any real impetus for innovation because of the existence of a large pool of labour. In short, as with the large contractor, but for somewhat different reasons, there are major obstacles to the adoption of appropriate technology by the small contractor.

4. **Rationale for appropriate technology in the private sector**

In section 2 of this chapter there was an examination of the environment within which the private sector operates, and the general conclusion reached was that government policies, contractual conditions, the attitudes of engineers and the functional divisions of the industry are not conducive to the application of appropriate technology. Similiarly, the section 3 analysis of the structure of the industry concluded that the existence of virtually only two categories of contractor, namely "large" and "small", was an inhibitng factor, and that, for different reasons, neither has any particular interest in appropriate technology.

Given these circumstances, two questions must be asked, or perhaps more strictly a main and a subsidiary question. The main question is this:

"*Should* appropriate technology be applied in the private sector?"

and the subsidiary question is

*"Can appropriate technology be applied in the private sector?"*

The answer to the first question must be a resounding yes, for the following reasons.

Whilst the capital for infrastructure development comes almost entirely from government sources and the management of projects rests largely with government departments, the actual execution of works is often in the hands of the private sector. There is a school of thought which maintains that the private contractor is a source of inefficiency, is guilty of exploiting labour and of making large profits, and that particularly on small-scale rural projects he should be eliminated. Without entering into the social/political controversies of which this is a reflection, it must be noted that in those cases where this has been done there is no evidence of improvement in either over-all efficiency or the lot of the workers. More compellingly, the fact remains that to attempt a wholesale change of the existing system as a necessary prelude to the introduction of appropriate technology would almost certainly end in failure. What the proponents of appropriate technology are saying is that its application offers the opportunity for the better use of human resources, and what we maintain is that this should be done within the system of project execution which is most commonly used throughout the region. Hence the positive answer to the first question.

As to the question of whether appropriate technology *can* be applied in the private sector, the answer here is yes — but .... In other words, a positive response, but a qualified one. Politics has been described, somewhat cynically, as the art of the possible; perhaps engineering should be described (but of course not cynically) as the science of the possible, since engineers are both realistic and practical. Therefore, practicability must be a paramount consideration in discussing the steps necessary to introduce appropriate technology into the private sector. This leads to the conclusion that attention should be concentrated on the small contractor. The large contractor is, in general, much more capable of taking care of himself than the small one, and in any event there are likely to be more serious technical problems in applying appropriate technology to large-scale than to small-scale works. Furthermore, development needs a healthy construction industry with a complete range of technical capacity. Appropriate technology provides a means of bridging the gap between the two extremes which presently characterises the private sector.

## 5. Action necessary to introduce appropriate technology in the private sector

There is scope for national action in the following fields, not only to remove constraints but to positively encourage the application of appropriate technology in the private sector.

### 5.1 *Legislation, regulations and conditions of contract*

Government recognition of the construction industry as such would enable the framing of laws and regulations appropriate to the industry. It would, so to speak, give it respectability and thus improve the status of private contractors, especially the small ones. Legislation and regulations could be framed which would make the contractor credit-worthy and thus able to use the tools and equipment of appropriate technology. The regulations which govern the registration of contractors could be amended so as to avoid a bias against labour-intensive methods.

Contractual conditions and specifications should be drawn up so as to allow the maximum possible choice of methodology. This is not a plea for the lowering of standards, but there are often alternative ways of producing the same end result, and specifications should not be so rigid as to permit of only one method.

The possibility should be investigated of writing conditions of contract which would offer the contractor an incentive for using labour-intensive methods, whilst at the same time maintaining productivity[6].

These matters would probably need to be dealt with nationally by some sort of committee or commission comprising professional engineers, lawyers, government officials, employers' and employees' associations.

### 5.2 *Research*

This is an important field in which, although a certain amount has been accomplished, a great deal more needs to be done. Both the ILO and the World Bank have been prominent in this field.

Most of the work to date has concentrated on demonstrating that, by using appropriate technology, the substitution of labour for capital is feasible, but there has been practically no investigation of the implications for the private sector. This work is now being extended by the ILO and the World Bank to cover the structure and organisation of the construction industry.

a) *The structure and organisation of the private sector* — At national levels there is an urgent need to determine what proportion of construction output is carried out by small contractors, how many of these there are, how many people they employ, how they operate, how permanent they are, what expertise they possess, and so forth. This kind of work can usually be undertaken by national bodies such as universities, technical institutes or business colleges.

One point that needs stressing is that research in this field should not be purely academic, but should be aimed at producing practical improvement. Thus analysis should only be regarded as a first step towards a programme of action.

b) *The use of physical resources by the private sector* This area can be further subdivided into:

    i) methodologies and techniques;
    ii) use of indigenous materials;
    iii) development of tools and equipment.

i) *Methodologies and techniques*: As stressed in the previous section, research should be directed towards improvement in the methods currently used. Most small contractors operate in ways which have been traditional for many years. Simple changes in organisation and methods can often increase productivity. Why does this not happen, and what can be done about it?

ii) *Use of indigenous materials*: A great deal of research has gone on, and is still going on, into the use of the local building materials, yet these materials are still not in general use. For such materials to be more widely adopted, a number of things must happen:

- the properties of the materials must be known and manufacturing standards must be drawn up;
- architects and engineers must specify their use;
- adequate and economically priced supplies must be available;

– contractors must know how to use the materials.

Responsibility for the first two rests largely with the government sector and is therefore outside the scope of this paper. The last two are within the private sector, however, and merit research into such matters as:

- the availability of raw materials;
- the economics of manufacture, including pricing structures, import substitution, etc.;
- the scale of manufacture;
- application techniques;
- construction costs.

The foregoing refer to the use of materials in permanent structures, but there is another research area which has been almost completely neglected, and that is the use of local materials for temporary structures. In practice, very little tubular steel scaffolding is used in Asia, most of it being bamboo or timber. Steel scaffolding, being a manufactured product, possesses predictable properties, yet there have recently been some spectacular failures, which would indicate that we know less about its behaviour than we thought[7]. How much smaller is our knowledge of the behaviour of bamboo or timber scaffolding? Not only is this important from the aspect of the safety of the structure and the workers thereon, but because the contractor must usually allow for the cost of these temporary strcutures in his price for the permanent structure. Similar research is needed into the use of local timber for the shoring of trench sides. This again is an item the cost of which is deemed to be included in the excavation price. Unfortunately, whereas a bridge or high building cannot be constructed without scaffolding, trenches can be dug without shoring, often with fatal results for the diggers.

iii) *Development of tools and equipment*: The ILO has started to compile a *Guide to Tools and Equipment for Labour-Based Road Construction*, and this is a useful first step, but the same entrepreneurial drive that has produced intermediate forms of transport needs to be harnessed at national level in the interest of construction equipment. This will require activity similar to that undertaken by the International Rice Research Institute in developing appropriate agricultural machinery, coupled with the creation of a market for the products by the encouragement of appropriate construction technology.

c) *The use of human and animal resources* — Reference has already been made to the studies carried out in this area by the World Bank and the ILO, and a particularly valuable output is the joint standard methodology for the measurement of productivity[8]. However, as these studies make clear, the variables affecting the output of men or animals are much more numerous than those affecting machines. It is therefore necessary that there should be continuing national research into productivity and the factors which affect it.

One of the vital factors is that of motivation and incentive, and here the research field is virtually untouched. Since this paper is concerned with the private sector, the assumption is that the motivation of the contractor is a desire to make a profit. This is perfectly legitimate, but the reason for advocating the application of appropriate technology is *not* primarily to allow him to make a large profit! It is to create employment, generate income and improve productivity, thereby benefiting all three parties, namely the government, the worker and the employer.

There have been many examples of the development of tools for increasing productivity which have never found acceptance. Why is this? The reasons are twofold:
  i) as has already been pointed out, in an environment where productivity is generally low, the contractors can still make an adequate profit without bothering to improve productivity.
  ii) the worker is naturally unwilling to increase his output if this is merely going to mean increased profits for his employer.

Socio-economic research is therefore needed to identify the factors governing the introduction of new tools and techniques into a contracting company, and to devise means of sharing the benefits in such a way as to encourage their adoption.

## 5.3 *Information*

The modern world devotes a great deal of effort and resources to the provision of more information, further information and more accurate information. In some cases, as for instance airline booking systems, this has resulted in noticeable improvements. On the other hand, the speed of delivery of letters often seems to be completely unaffected by technological advances. In general terms, however, our ability to process data into information more readily than our predecessors at least gives us the opportunity to manage our resources better. Whether or not we grasp that opportunity is another matter. Consideration of the techniques to be used for the supply of information is beyond the scope of this paper, but here is a situation where the appropriate technology may well be the most advanced technology available. If, for example, the logistics of supplying scattered rural works projects are helped by the provision of radio communication, this is a more appropriate technology than that of a runner with a cleft stick, even though the projects themselves may use very little equipment.

As far as the private sector is concerned, there are two categories of information required, namely external and internal. By the former is meant information which relates to the political, social and economic environment within which the contractor operates. It is this kind of information which creates an awareness of the availability of alternative technologies, of the social responsibilities of management, and so on. Arising from this awareness there should spring the need for the second category of information, which is that relating to the internal operation of the contractor's business. This will include cost and productivity analyses, progress reports, and so forth. The contractor who is not generally aware of what is going on around him is unlikely to have a highly developed internal information system.

The large contractor, because of the size of projects he is undertaking and his technical contacts, has access to a great deal of information. Of course, much of this will be biased towards capital-intensive technologies because of the magazines and brochures produced by equipment manufactures, but he is at least attuned to the concept of receiving new ideas, so that literature relating to appropriate technology would at least receive some attention. Furthermore, many large contractors are organised into federations or associations which allow the interchange of ideas both nationally and internationally. Therefore, information relating to appropriate technology can be disseminated through existing channels.

The case of the small contractor is, however, completely different. As far as external information is concerned, there are a number of serious problems:

a) that of language. Whereas the large contractor will be able to read literature in at least one of the world's major languages, the small contractor may not be able to do so;

b) availability of suitable information. A great deal needs to be done in the structure of the private sector, the systems whereby it operates, and so on. Our lack of factual knowledge regarding small contractors is abysmal. Until this situation is corrected, it is difficult to know what external information the small contractor needs;

c) lack of managerial and technical know-how. Even if suitable external information in his own language were made available to the small contractor, he would probably not be able to formulate his needs for internal information due to these limitations;

d) cost of information. Small contractors simply cannot afford publications printed at high cost in the western world.

What can be done to solve these problems? An obvious first step is the identification of the information needs of the small contractor, followed by consideration of the best means of fulfilling those needs. It would appear that the research needed for this first step could provide an opportunity for regional or at least subregional co-operation, since there are many similarities between the way small contractors operate in say the subcontinent of India or in the ASEAN countries. The carrying out of some such research programme would not, however, solve the problem of making the information available to the contractor in his own language and at a reasonable cost. Patently the necessary steps for this to happen would have to be taken at country level and should preferably involve a national institution: it might be a national productivity centre, or a rural development academy, or an engineering faculty of a university.

What the foregoing amounts to is that if appropriate technology is to be adopted by small contractors they must have ways of knowing about it. Since information channels for this purpose are restricted or non-existent, positive steps are needed to remedy this. The kind of information needed can probably be established on a regional or subregional basis, but the channels of communication will need to be set up at the country level.

## 5.4 *Training*

As has already been seen, there are many external factors which require influencing if appropriate technology is to be successfully introduced into the private sector of consturction. Changes are also necessary within the industry itself in the form of better information and control systems, improved managerial and supervisory capability, greater technical know-how. Some of these improvements can be wrought by the provision of suitable training, but whilst there are few, if any, contractors whose performance is not susceptible to improvement through training, the need is greatest amongst the small contractors. Additionally, it is in this category that the greatest potential exists for the productive use of appropriate technology. For these reasons, the discussion that follows concentrates on training for small contractors, whose general needs fall into the three categories:

   a) management and organisation;
   b) finance;
   c) technical.

For a contractor employed on small-scale works, his training needs in the fields of estimating, costing, financial control and the running of a small business generally are independent of the construction technology employed. However, the application of appropriate technology does involve some special management issues such as:

   — methods of payment, especially where work animals are used;
   — incentive schemes;
   — measurement and control of productivity;
   — training of workers in the use of tools and equipment.

As regards the need for technical training, it is self-evident that the introduction of a technology different from that currently used by the contractor involves teaching him how to manage it, and his labour how to handle the equipment.

When it comes to the mechanisms whereby training is to be imparted to the small contractor, it is the author's view that the training needs which arise directly from the application of appropriate technology cannot be separated from those arising from any other reason. The small contractor needs training which will raise his general standard of competence. For him, *appropriate* training will include not only appropriate technology but general business management, simple accounting, planning, and so forth. There are a number of special problems to be overcome if this training is to be effective.

In the first place, there is very little training in construction management available in Asia for small contractors such as there is for the large contractor. A start has been made in Malaysia, with technical assistance from the ILO, to develop within an existing institution, a training programme specifically for small-scale contractors, but this is thought to be the first attempt in the whole region. Programmes will therefore need to be developed from scratch with no past experience for guidance.

Secondly, only a few studies have been carried out on the characteristics of these small-scale contractors[9]: what education and technical training have they had? What do they know of business management? What permanent staff do they employ? How do they pay their casual labourers? And so on. Until there is more information, it is difficult to design a suitable training programme.

Thirdly, there is often little permanence amongst these contractors. Reference has already been made to the use by governments of the construction industry as an economic regulator, so that when the supply of projects is cut off, many contractors go out of business, and conversely new ones may emerge when there is economic growth. Additionally, whilst a large contractor will not find it difficult to release a member of his staff for training, the small contractor may be an owner/manager, engineer, storekeeper all rolled into one, and therefore cannot afford to neglect his business whilst he receives training. A related problem is largely psychological: the type of contractor under discussion is obviously an entrepreneur and may be suspicious of formal training, especially if it is not immediately obvious how he is to benefit financially.

Finally, any training programme for this target group must be in the local language, and since the literature even for "standard" subjects such as accounting is unlikely to exist in that language, the translation problems are formidable.

In the context of this chapter it is not possible to do more than sketch some possible solutions, but a long and difficult path must be trodden before success is achieved. It is of prime importance to know and understand the target group for training, and this can only be achieved through national studies. As part of its research under the World Employment Programme the ILO has initiated a study in the Philippines and will be carrying out similar studies in various other Asian countries. These efforts are very useful in providing models for future work, but conditions vary so widely from country to country and even within countries that specific country studies will be needed throughout the region.

The almost total lack of existing training is a strong argument for using existing technical institutions which already possess training competence, since this is a necessary foundation on which to build. Such institutions should have an engineering and practical orientation, otherwise they will possess little credibility with their trainees. Another argument for using local institutions is that they will understand local conditions and needs, and will also conduct their training in the local language.

Now, although every country will ultimately have to develop its own programmes, for it to do so in isolation without drawing on expertise and experience from elsewhere will be too long and wasteful a process in the light of its pressing development needs. One way of solving this problem would be for international assistance to be given to groups of institutions in the preparation of training packets and the training of instructors. This could be done by bringing together instructors from a number of institutions within a large country (such as India), or from a group of smaller countries (such as the ASEAN) and helping them to develop a generalised training packet which they would subsequently adapt to local requirements. The ILO has made a start in Africa by running a six-week regional training course to teach management trainers from 18 countries how to deliver a basic repertoire of courses to small-scale building and construction contractors. The author has proposed something on similar lines for Asia, but with continuing help to the national institutions on a longer-term basis, and with provision for interchange of know-how and experience between institutions themselves.

These ideas are by no means exhaustive and there may well be other and perhaps better ways of tackling the training problems, but the subject is one worthy of an exploration in depth which cannot be attempted here.

## 6. Summary and conclusions

The role of the private construction industry in the development of the countries of Asia and the Pacific is a vital one, since it is the means by which most governments execute their projects. A healthy and efficient industry is therefore in the interests of both governments and contractors. It is, however, also in the interest of construction workers for whom there can be greater employment prospects and improved earnings.

The private sector is presently characterised by an imbalance between the relatively small number of large contractors, modelled on their counterparts in industrialised countries, and the many thousands of small contractors trapped in a sequence of primitive technology, low productivity, hence low wages leading back full circle to primitive technology. It is necessary to break this circle and encourage the creation of a middle category of contractor which will bridge the gap between large and small. This will enable the more enterprising amongst the small contractors to move upwards. Appropriate technology affords one means whereby this natural growth can be achieved. It follows that efforts in the field of appropriate technology should concentrate on improving the performance of the small contractor.

In order to do this, it is necessary to consider the environment within which the industry operates, as well as the structure of the industry itself. Since government has a monopoly of the market for the small contractor, it is government policies which control the operating environment. The legislation, regulations and conditions of contract which relate to the construction industry must therefore be examined and amended as necessary in order to encourage the upgrading of the small contractor. There is also a need to reduce the intellectual and technical gap between government engineers and contractors, so that there is greater understanding of each other's problems.

As regards the industry itself, there is a dearth of statistical data, and research is needed to provide a realistic foundation on which to build a sound structure. If he is to apply new ideas and technologies, the contractor must have access to information. This must be simple, available cheaply and in his own language. Finally, the small contractor needs training if his standards are to be raised. Since these are generally low, the training should not concentrate on appropriate technology alone, but should include it in a general syllabus. The more aware the contractor becomes of relevant management and technical techniques the more likely he is to innovate. International assistance should be given to suitable national institutions to enable them to introduce training for small contractors.

This paper has spelled out in some detail the formidable, but none the less surmountable, obstacles which impede the adoption of appropriate technology in the private sector. What it is hoped has emerged is that obstacles are an impediment not only to the adoption of appropriate technology but to the progress which the construction industry must achieve if it is to meet the challenge of development. There must therefore be a concerted effort on the part of all concerned, whether in the public or private sectors, to tackle the problems.

**Notes and references**

[1] *Employment relationship in the building industry* by C.K. Johri and S.M. Pandey. Published by Shri Ram Centre for Industrial Relations and Human Resources, New Delhi.

[2] op. cit.

[3] IBRD, *Study of the Substitution of Labour and Equipment in Civil Construction*. Transportation Department, World Bank, Phase I, 1971.

[4] *1976 World Population Data*, Population Reference Bureau, Washington DC.

[5] G.W. Irvin, *Roads and redistribution - social costs and benefits of labour-intensive road construction in Iran*, ILO, Geneva, 1975.

[6] This has been attempted in the Philippines. See D. Lal, *Men or machines*, op. cit.

[7] 1976 saw the failure of temporary bridge structures in Germany

and Britain, and a failure during construction at the Montreal Olympic Stadium.

[8] IBRD/ILO, Technical Memorandum No. 8, *A Field Manual for the Collection of Productivity Data from Civil Construction Projects*.

[9] See, for instance, J. Capt and G.A. Edmonds, "Small contractors in Kenya", WEP Technology and Employment Working Paper No. 33 (mimeo.), Jan. 1978.

# PART II  CASE STUDIES

## CHAPTER 6. THE "ROADS AND LABOUR" PROGRAMME, MEXICO[1]

### by G.A. Edmonds

In 1971 the Mexican Government launched an extremely ambitious programme of rural road construction. The primary objective of this programme was to provide communication to the mass of the rural population where presently none existed[1].

At the time of the inception of the programme it was estimated that as many as 12 million people (60 per cent of the rural population) living in a total of 16,000 villages had no proper transport access[2]. Whilst the major transportation links had been constructed there had been little attention paid to providing the necessary minor roads without which the rural areas were incapable of developing effectively. It was the intention therefore to reverse the ratio of the kilometrage of major to minor roads during the period of the programme. Thus in 1971 80 per cent of the roads already constructed were major trunk roads. By a massive programme of labour-based road construction it was hoped to reduce this value to 20 per cent. This implied the construction of some 150,000 kms of minor roads.

The major objective of the programme therefore was to provide communication to the mass of the population. However, it was decided that a policy of labour-based construction would be adopted not only to provide employment and income but also because this policy was geared to popular and grass-roots participation in the construction process. The programme was not conceived therefore as a public works scheme to generate employment but as an effective means of providing access to markets and amenities to a large proportion of the rural population. As with the Ministry of Works in Kenya, the Secretaría de Obras Públicas, who are responsible for the programme, wished to use labour-based methods to the extent that they were commensurate with technical and economic efficiency.

1. **Programme organisation and administration**

In the capital town of every state in Mexico there is a centre of the Secretaría de Obras Públicas (Secretary of Public Works). Its director is responsible for all public works carried out by the federal government in that state. In each centre there is a senior resident engineer who is in charge of the construction of rural roads[3]. Working for him is a team of resident engineers each located in a different region of the state. Each resident engineer has a team of engineers, surveyors, administrative personnel and supervisory staff. The exact number of his staff depends upon the number of roads being planned or constructed. The supervisory staff consists of supervisors and foremen. Supervisors are in charge of 3 to 5 foremen, whilst each foreman is in charge of 30 to 60 men.

The central headquarters of the programme is located in Mexico City in the Secretaría de Obras Públicas (SOP). A special unit has been set up to supervise the programme (Dirección General de Caminos Rurales). This unit consists of four main departments. These are:

*Department of Works* — responsible for monitoring the progress and cost of the programme and advising when action is necessary.

*Department of Programming* — responsible for preparing the budget and allocating funds to the SOP centres in the various states.

*Technical Department* — responsible for supervision of the technical aspects of the programme. This includes drawing up guidelines on technical specifications, cost estimates for labour, materials, equipment, etc. and productivity standards. It also collects data from the field in order to update these guidelines.

*Department of Research and Special Studies* — responsible for carrying out special studies on technical and economic aspects of the programme. In addition there is what is termed a promotion branch which is responsible for giving advice and assistance to the resident engineers in the field as regards the promotion within local communities of road-building activities.

This is necessary because the programme is dependent upon, and derives from, the willingness of local communities to become involved in road construction.

In the first instance a community will request that a road be built or upgraded. One of the resident engineer's staff then visits the community, assesses the situation and collects data pertaining to the number of households, agricultural production, social services, etc. If a decision is then taken to meet the community's request the official returns and explains that it is their responsibility to build and maintain the road. To this end a committee is elected which represents the community in its dealings with the resident engineer's office. A memorandum of understanding is drawn up in which the obligations of the two parties are clearly spelled out. Thus the committee undertakes to provide the necessary manpower; the free use of borrow pits and the right of way for the road. The DGCR undertakes to provide technical assistance, payment for the labourers, construction materials, hand tools, equipment and transport.

Two points are worth mentioning here. First, the system is designed to ensure the involvement of the community in the construction of the road, which it is hoped will guarantee its maintenance. Second, the DGCR has no official relations with the labourers except in terms of supervising the construction operations. The workers are paid by the committee and all labour relations are dealt with by them. The labourers therefore are not in any way employees of the Government. In a programme as large as this one decentralisation of administrative responsibility presents major problems of accounting and planning. To help to cope with these problems each SOP centre has a computer which is used to plan and control the financial disbursements of the programme. In turn the information from all the SOP centres is fed to the main computing centre at SOP headquarters which allows the Department of Works and Department of Programming to monitor and allocate the financial resources.

## 2. **Technical aspects**

### 2.1 *Design*

It was assumed that the traffic volume on the roads to be

constructed would be less than 50 vehicles/day. The roads were therefore designed to a design speed of only 20 – 30 kms per hour. This permits the use of radius of curvature as little as 15 – 20 m and maximum over-all gradient of 12 per cent.

The roads are designed for one-way traffic flow. The total formation width is 4.6 m with a 4.0 m wide, 15 cms deep gravel pavement. Every 500 m a 10 m stretch is widened to 6.0 m to allow vehicles to pass.

On simple rural roads, drainage is particularly important. This has been appreciated in the programme and special attention is given to it. The formation is crowned with a cross-fall of 4 per cent. Side drains of 1 m width and 1:3 side slopes are constructed. These have a minimum gradient of 0.5 per cent and where the gradient exceeds 6 per cent they are protected with a layer of hard pitched stone. On sloping ground catch drains are placed on the high side of the road to discharge run-off water before it reaches the road. Various culvert designs have been introduced but the most effective has proved to be corruged steel pipe.

To the extent possible, rivers and streams have been traversed by means of masonry fords. Where bridges have been necessary they were initially constructed as masonry arches. Recently however masonry pillars and reinforced concrete superstructure have been introduced. One interesting aspect has been the use of cobblestone roads where the gradient was unavoidably greater than 12 per cent.

## 2.2 *Construction*

Prior to construction work commencing the resident engineer and his staff prepare a simple bill of quantities which specifies the amount of work to be carried out in each of the major activities. This is then used to plan the work in terms of duration and resource requirements. This is possible because the reporting system incorporated into the programme provides detailed information on labour and equipment productivity under various climatic, topographical and soil conditions.

The resident engineer's team then sets out the centre line of the road. Tasks for each of the major activities are then fixed. These tasks generally cover a 3 to 4-day period. Each foreman, who is in charge of 30 to 40 labourers, is briefed regarding the task levels set and any particular points that need attention. In turn he assigns his labourers to the various tasks.

Site clearance and top soil removal is almost always carried out by manual methods except (in the case of site clearance) when the vegetation is extremely dense.

The roads are designed and aligned to minimise cut and fill operations and to ensure that, in general, the excavated material for side drains and culverts can be used directly to form the basic road formation. Thus the material from ditching and sloping is used for spreading on the formation. This means that these operations can be carried out effectively by labour-intensive methods.

Where bulk excavation is unavoidable it has been found that labour-intensive methods are effective as long as the total volume does not exceed 2,500 m$^3$ per kilometre[4]. Where this figure is exceeded equipment is used. This is often operated by small contractors who are paid a fixed sum related to the type of soil being excavated.

Gravel for the pavement is obtained from borrow pits. Excavation and loading of the gravel is carried out either by labour or equipment depending on location, material and loading conditions. Dump trucks are used for hauling the material. Spreading and laying is carried out entirely by hand.

## 2.3 *Tools*

Each labourer is provided with a shovel and a pick-axe. Other hand tools such as crowbars, axes, hammers, etc. are distributed according to the type of activities being executed. The tools are produced in Mexico and their quality is very reasonable. For haul distances of up to 100 m wheelbarrows are used. The wheelbarrows used have a capacity of 0.07 to 0.09 m$^3$ and have massive rubber tyres.

## 2.4 *Recruitment and remuneration*

The community itself recruits the labour to work on the roads. Each labourer is guaranteed a minimum of two week's work. (In fact during the period 1971-75 53 per cent of the workers were employed for less than one month, 21 per cent for one to three months and 26 per cent for more than three months.) In general the community committee attempts to ensure that all those who wish to work are given some employment.

Payment is usually at the level of the minimum rural wage, with one paid rest day per week. During the period 1972-75 the minimum rural wage rose from 25.38 pesos ($2) in 1972 to 40.89 pesos ($3.27) in 1975. The present rate of remuneration is approximately 70 pesos per day ($3.1). The actual direct cost of labour is a factor of 1.167 greater per day owing to payment for one rest day per week.

## 2.5 *General*

Some general indications can be given of the 64,000 kms of road already constructed under the programme. Only 14 per cent of the roads are in fact new roads, the great majority being improvements to the alignment, width, drainage and surfacing of existing tracks. The average length of the roads constructed is 10 kms and average construction period 9½ months.

The topography in which the roads have been constructed was classified in three categories, i.e. plain, hilly and mountainous[5]. Only 7.5 per cent of the roads were constructed in mountainous terrain, the rest being equally distributed between plain and hilly terrain.

The type of soil was classified into three types: soft, firm and hard. Nearly 60 per cent of the soils encountered were firm, 35 per cent soft and the remainder were hard. The vegetation through which the roads were constructed was generally (50 per cent) medium in density, a further 40 per cent was very light, whilst 10 per cent of the roads were constructed through jungle or forest.

## 2.6 *Selection of roads*

With such a large programme of road construction it was necessary to develop certain criteria of selection.

It was decided to concentrate road-building efforts on those communities of 500 – 2,500 population of which 65 per cent had no means of communication. This would provide access to the major part of 12 million people mentioned previously.

An initial, broad, identification was made to decide which

states in the country should be given priority. The criteria used for this broad selection were:
a) level of rural income;
b) number of localities between 300 and 800 inhabitants;
c) metres of constructed road per square kilometre of land surface;
d) metres of constructed road per 1,000 inhabitants;
e) number of vehicles per 1,000 inhabitants.

Actual project selection within each state was carried out based on certain specific criteria which related to maximising the "combined utility of the road". This was measured in terms of:
a) number of localities served by the road;
b) potential agricultural development;
c) permanent employment generated by construction of the road;
d) general socio-economic level;
e) zone of influence of the road.

The selection was qualified by such factors as budget restrictions, availability of labour, duration of construction and the technical difficulty of construction.

## 3. **Achievements**

3.1 *General*

During the five-year period 1971 – 75, 64,000 kms of road have been built at a total cost of 4,596 million pesos ($368 million). That is an average cost of $5,750 per kilometre. The total length of roads built under the programme amounts to 35 per cent of the length of the current road network in Mexico. In all, 6,174 communities with a total population of some 6 million have been provided with access. At its peak in 1973 the programme was providing temporary employment of 105,000 jobs per month. A rough calculation based on the time (relatively short) that workers spent on road construction suggests that over 1.5 million people were provided with temporary employment during the five-year period up to 1975.

3.2 *Output*

The actual construction output has varied considerably over

the five years 1971 – 75 as shown below:

| Year | Output (kms) |
|---|---|
| 1971 | 3 500 |
| 1972 | 11 000 |
| 1973 | 28 500 |
| 1974 | 10 500 |
| 1975 | 10 500 |
| Total | 64 000 |

A weighted average of the programmes indicates that 1,700 man-days per kilometre were used.

Detailed figures of labour productivity for various activities are shown in table 1 and a breakdown of the average quantity of work per kilometre is given in table 2.

*Table 1. Labour productivity*

| Operation | Soil type | Output ($m^3$/man-day) |
|---|---|---|
| Cut to fill | Soft | 4.5 |
| | Firm | 3.0 |
| | Hard | 1.2 |
| Simple excavations | Soft | 5.0 |
| | Firm | 3.0 |
| | Hard | 1.2 |
| Spreading | All | 15.0 |

*Table 2. Average quantity of material per kilometre constructed*

| Operation | Average quantity per kilometre | |
|---|---|---|
| | Improved track | New road |
| Clearing | 0.3 hectares | 1 hectare |
| Excavation | 1 670 $m^3$ | 2 800 $m^3$ |
| Fill | 1 313 $m^3$ | 1 415 $m^3$ |
| Gravel | 710 $m^3$ | 815 $m^3$ |

## 3.3 *Costs*

During the period 1972 – 74, for which a detailed analysis

has been carried out, the average direct costs for improvement of an existing track was 65,600 pesos per kilometre ($5,250) and for a new road 106,885 pesos per kilometre ($8,550).

For the bulk of the roads, which were improved tracks, the breakdown of costs was as follows:

| | |
|---|---|
| Wages | 60% |
| Materials | 12% |
| Tools | 4.5% |
| Services[6] | 20% |
| Site supervision | 3.5% |

The cost and breakdown does not include the cost of central administration and headquarters which, in the case of the Mexican programme, is likely to have been quite considerable.

During this period (1972 – 74) the average minimum daily wage was 41 pesos. An analysis of the costs in 1975 shows[7] that the direct costs per kilometre for an improved track had risen to 93,500 pesos ($7,500).

Over-all it is estimated that of the direct cost 50 per cent is spent on earthworks, 3 per cent on drainage and 3 per cent on the gravelling operation.

A comparison was made of the costs of constructing an improved track by equipment-intensive methods under prevailing Mexican conditions[8]. This suggested that, even at market prices, there was little difference between labour and equipment even though the duration of construction for the equipment-intensive techniques was considerably less. It is worth noting that the on-site overheads for the equipment-intensive method (a total of 23.5 per cent of the total direct cost in the case of labour-based methods) was 33 per cent of the total direct cost.

3.4 *Employment*

The actual level of direct employment created is difficult to quantify as at least half of the workers were employed for less than a month. From the available figures[9] it is possible to suggest (i) that over 1.5 million people were provided with employment as a direct result of the road construction programme; (ii) during the period 1972 – 74 over 4 million man-months of employment were created.

Employment created using labour-based methods was five times that which could have been expected using equipment and, as we have seen above, for the same investment cost.

Van Ginneken[10] has estimated that of the 5 million paid economically active persons in agriculture as many as 4 million are employed for less than 150 days a year. This should be seen in relation to the structure of agricultural employment which is basically of four types. The day-labourer having little or no land who hires himself out for work through the year; the co-operative farmer whose demand for employment depends upon the distribution of crop land; the small farmer (having less than five hectares) whose subsistence farming is often augmented by working as a day-labourer; large farmers. Employment in the programme was drawn from the first three. We can see therefore that even if a labourer works for only one month on the road he is, at the most conservative estimate, increasing his annual employment by 20 per cent, and consequently his earnings.

A sample survey which formed part of the work of the DGCR showed that three-quarters of the labourers working on the road had access to land; however, the average size of plot was only 2.9 hectares. This is extremely small when it is appreciated that the average family size was 6.3 and of the total family, an average of 3.6 were available for work. In over 90 per cent of the families all or part of the family labour force was available for work (i.e. unemployed or underemployed).

The average annual income of the families studied was approximately 7,000 pesos[11] which amounts to an annual income per economically active person of 2,000 pesos. One month's employment on the programme therefore amounted to an increase of 50 per cent in individual income or 15 per cent of family income.

A micro survey carried out by DGCR suggested that it was the day-labourers who benefited most from the programme whilst those who had land (not surprisingly) and the totally unemployed (surprisingly) benefited much less.

## 4. Socio-economic impact

Up to 1975 the programme had provided access to over 6,000 communities. A sample survey of these communities showed that:
    a) for 70 per cent of them the only previous means of communication was on foot or by horse;

b) for the great majority the time taken to reach the nearest town was at least one hour and generally more than three hours;
c) 37 per cent lacked all types of services, 70 per cent had no potable water, 60 per cent no electricity, 60 per cent no school of any description, 90 per cent no medical service.

The survey also showed that over 90 per cent of the wages earned by workers on the programme was spent on consumption items.

The direct socio-economic impact of the construction of the roads was therefore an increase, in most cases a substantial increase, in family income. Unfortunately, because of the existing lack of facilities and the economic system this income was generally not spent in the communities but in towns to the merchants who supply basic commodities. The addition of funds to the community did not produce an increase in the local production of consumer goods. It is fair to add that this would only come about if complementary rural development activities took place at the same time as the road construction. Furthermore, the DGCR found that the improved communication provided by the roads tended to reinforce the existing economic structure. The richer members of the communities took advantage of the access provided whilst the poorer members, because of their lack of income, derived very little benefit from the access. Thus a richer family would now have access to fertiliser which they could afford and thus increase the quality and quantity of crops produced. The income derived by the poorest, though relatively substantial, was only used to increase consumption, partially because the previous consumption was so low and partly because of the class structure which did not allow them to break out of their subsistence economy. Thus the additional income provided the means whereby the basic needs of clothing, food and shelter could be obtained but were not sufficient to provide a basis for a continuing improvement in the people's economic condition. In this regard the survey found that the least impact occurred when the class structure was particularly rigid and land ownership vested in the hands of a few.

5. **Summary**
The programme is probably the largest of its kind presently in

operation. It has indicated clearly that even in economies where the agricultural wage rate is as high as $2.5, labour-based methods can be effective. However, it also shows that these methods require very detailed planning, organisation and management.

The detailed studies carried out by the DGCR have also shown that for a programme of rural road construction to be truly effective in the long term it must be accompanied by complementary rural development activities. If not then improvements to the standard of living of the mass of the population are unlikely to be achieved.

**Notes and references**

[1] This chapter is based on the various publications of the Secretaría de Obras Públicas, Mexico, related to this programme, in particular Secretaría de Obras Públicas, *Caminos y de Mano de Obra*, Mexico 1977.

[2] Defined as having no year-round access to a truckable road.

[3] It is interesting to compare this system with the RARP in Kenya where the RAR engineers are not part of the Provincial Engineers Organisation but report directly to the Central Headquarters.

[4] A similar conclusion has been reached from the Kenyan RARP.

[5] The classification was designated if more than 60 per cent of the road was in one type of terrain.

[6] This is principally transportation costs.

[7] SOP, *op. cit.*

[8] ibid.

[9] SOP, op. cit.

[10] W. Van Ginneken, *Socio-economic groups in Mexico: a study of income distribution and employment*, forthcoming ILO publication.

[11] This implies a per capita income of 1,100 pesos which should be compared with the *national* per capita income at the time of the survey of 11,000 pesos.

# CHAPTER 7. THE SELF-HELP APPROACH: AFGHANISTAN

*by G. Glaister*

## 1. Introduction

This chapter describes a major programme of labour-based construction in Afghanistan. Unlike the programmes in Kenya, Philippines, India and Mexico referred to elsewhere, this programme is based on the principle of self-help, that is, the workers donate their services free or for the provision of food. Nevertheless the objective is not primarily the generation of employment but the development of rural infrastructure.

In Afghanistan there are two major agencies engaged in the construction and maintenance of roads. These are:
a) the Ministry of Public Works;
b) the Rural Development Department.

The former is responsible for primary and secondary roads and the latter for tertiary roads. In this context primary roads are defined as those connecting the provincial capitals with the centre (Kabul) and with the major international border crossing points and points of entry. Secondary roads are defined as those connecting the district capitals with the provincial capitals either directly or via the primary road system. Tertiary roads are defined as those connecting villages and other centres of production or marketing with the primary and secondary road systems.

The construction of the primary road system is well advanced and of the 27 provincial capitals, 17 are served by asphalt or concrete, two-lane, all-weather roads, 4 are served by good quality all-weather gravel roads and the other 6 by lower-grade earth or gravel roads which may be impassable in the wet season because of high water levels.

The secondary road system is much less developed and all-weather secondary roads are the exception. The bulk of them are low-grade earth tracks with few bridges or other drainage structures. A number of district capitals are not connected by road.

The tertiary road system consists in the main of earth tracks which are frequently impassable during the wet season.

The Ministry of Public Works is concentrating on completing the primary road system and the more important secondary roads. It uses relatively equipment-intensive methods with the bulk of the labour being provided by the "Labour Corps", a unit of the Afghan army.

The Rural Development Department (RDD) uses entirely labour-based methods. The policy of the department obliges it to use voluntary unskilled labour sometimes supported by food assistance from the World Food Programme (WFP).

## 2. **The Rural Development Department (RDD)**

More than 85 per cent of the population of Afghanistan lives in the rural areas and the basic economy of the country depends on their productivity.

The Rural Development Department provides direct assistance to village people to carry out schemes for which they themselves felt the need and to which they were prepared to give their labour and other resources. The basic policy of the RDD is therefore to help villagers to help themselves. This does not mean that it adopts a passive role. On the contrary, it adopts an active leadership role in stimulating ideas in the villages, discussing and identifying their needs and helping them to plan for themselves. The planning process, socio-economic survey and technical survey is carried out in close consultation with the villagers themselves. For example, the location of a road or the siting of a bridge is discussed with the village and if there are technical reasons for a particular location these technical reasons are explained to the villagers and their general agreement is obtained. No decision is imposed on a village and if agreement cannot be reached the project is not usually undertaken. The RDD provides assistance to a village on the understanding that the village itself will contribute its own resources to the project in terms of voluntary labour, local materials and sometimes a cash contribution. In this way the execution of the project is very much a joint effort and when it is completed the villagers consider it as their project.

## 2.1 *Organisation structure*

The RDD is headed by a President with two Vice-Presidents, one in charge of the technical side of the department and the other in charge of administration. Under the technical Vice-President are four general directorates. These are:
   a) Director-General, Planning and Programming: in charge of over-all planning, programming, budgeting and monitoring of all departmental activities both technical and non-technical.
   b) Director-General, Technical Planning: in charge of all technical planning from the project initiation stage to the production of final drawings and estimates.
   c) Director-General, Social Services and Agriculture: in charge of non-engineering programmes in agriculture, non-formal education, health, co-operatives, rural industries, etc.
   d) Director-General, Construction: in charge of construction of roads, buildings, irrigation structures and canals, domestic water supplies, individual bridges, foot bridges, culverts, etc.

The RDD headquarters sends teams into the field to carry out socio-economic surveys, technical surveys and construction.

The initiation of projects takes the form of a request from the village to the provincial office of the RDD. The procedure is as follows:
   a) a request is made from the village to the RDD provincial office;
   b) the village is visited by a technician from the RDD provincial office who identifies the necessary local contribution of labour and materials;
   c) the request is forwarded to RDD headquarters by the RDD provincial office with the information gathered in (b) and the recommendations of the RDD provincial Director and the Governor;
   d) a socio-economic survey team from RDD headquarters visits the village and appraises the project;

e) if the project is considered viable a technical survey team from RDD headquarters surveys the site;
f) the project is designed in RDD headquarters and, subject to final technical and financial appraisal, is approved;
g) a mobile construction team from RDD headquarters is assigned to provide construction supervision and management, transport, eqipment, non-local materials and certain categories of skilled labour not available locally.

The construction team would be supplemented by voluntary unskilled labour provided by the village or villages and paid skilled labour either from the village or the nearby locality. The construction team lives on the site either in accommodation provided by the village or in tents. The construction team has administrative support from, and is supplied through, the provincial RDD office which is also responsible for seeing that the construction team gets the labour which has been promised by the village. If necessary the RDD Provincial Director will call on the assistance of the Provincial Governor to ensure this.

The construction equipment and transport available to these teams is extremely limited. This equipment is maintained by a small central workshop in Kabul which has inadequate resources to provide any field services except to nearby provinces. The RDD is procuring a considerable quantity of basic construction equipment. This is being financed from both Afghan, bilateral and multilateral sources, the total expected to be procured in the next two or three years amounting to about $3 million. This equipment is of two basic types:

a) To equip road and irrigation construction teams to enable better quality to be achieved and more economic design criteria adopted. These teams will operate on a labour-based basis, equipment and transport being provided only for those operations which are difficult or impossible by hand methods, e.g. rock drills, dump trucks, concrete vibrators and mixers, pumps, back hoes for deep excavation, etc.

Three road teams and two irrigation teams are planned to operate in the more backward and thinly populated

provinces whose development requires particular attention.
b) Basic equipment for general use throughout the 27 provinces of Afghanistan. This equipment consists in the main of concrete mixers and vibrators and pumps.

A central workshop and mobile field teams are being set up to service this equipment.

The RDD has 27 field offices at provincial level. These offices provide liaison services between the provincial government, the villages and RDD headquarters. They generate new projects and are in constant direct touch with the villagers analysing their needs and suggesting solutions to their problems. These provincial offices also organise all local resource inputs to construction programmes and other RDD activities. They are responsible for the administrative and supply back-up to the construction teams.

In the longer term it is intended to decentralise the technical operation of the department to the provincial offices. At the present time however there is insufficient technical staff to be able to do this, the department having only 34 engineers to cover administration, management and technical functions.

Construction supervisors are recruited to RDD as 12th grade school leavers. They undergo a four months' course in construction methods at the RDD training institute at Gulzar near Kabul. This course is very basic and practical in nature. A construction handbook in Farsi has been prepared and forms the basis of the course. The course includes instruction on reading simple drawings, setting out, simple measurements of areas and volumes, the techniques of mixing and placing concrete, building in random rubble masonry and brickwork, the construction of simple formwork and falsework, etc. It also includes basic instruction in keeping simple site records and organising labour. On completion of their course they are assigned to a construction team to gain practical field experience. Refresher courses are held from time to time.

## 3. **Construction resources**

In any labour-based programme the major resource utilised is labour and, when voluntary or semi-voluntary labour is used, the well spring of this resource is motivation. The identification of this motivation and the means of sustaining it therefore

becomes a major consideration in the planning process. Three types of unskilled labour, entirely confined to males, are in regular employment on RDD schemes:
a) voluntary labour;
b) voluntary labour supplemented by food rations;
c) labour supplemented by food rations plus a small cash payment. (The value of the food ration plus the cash is always less than the ruling rate for paid labour.)

The motivation of the purely voluntary labour is the desire for access to the national transport system. The villagers of Afghanistan are acutely aware of the economic benefits arising from cheaper transport. In most cases the farmers are owner occupiers who have a farm surplus to export from their area. They are fully aware of the price differentials between the farm gate, the district market, the provincial market and the national market and the effect of transport costs and middlemen's margins on these price differentials. The motivation is therefore mainly economic although there is a growing awareness of the social benefits which can accrue. For example it is most difficult for a village to attract and keep a good school teacher if it is not connected by a road.

In the case of roads which serve a number of villages the incentive to provide purely voluntary labour varies with the location of the actual worksite relative to the location of the village. For example, in the case of a bridge those villagers living on the near side of the river have little or no incentive to construct the bridge as the benefits will go to villages located on the far side of the river. Where a village is located close to and on the near side of the bridge the villagers are a very convenient potential source of labour; however, if no benefits accrue to them they will not provide voluntary labour. The villagers living on the far side of the river who stand to benefit from the bridge may live a considerable distance away and it may not be feasible for them to travel to the worksite each day. In such cases it has been found necessary to provide an additional incentive to the villagers on the near side of the river to provide labour for the construction. This incentive usually takes the form of food rations provided by WFP. In some cases, where this incentive does not produce the necessary labour, a cash incentive is paid in addition to the food. This cash incentive usually amounts to 20 per cent of the going wage rate.

Similar considerations apply to the construction of individual lengths of road which form parts of a complete road. Thus, on a particular length, all three types of labour, voluntary, WFP supported and WFP plus cash supported, may be working in the same gang at the same time; the proportion of each type depending on the benefits which that particular length of road will provide to each individual group.

Indigenous materials such as random rubble masonry, stone, gravel and sand aggregates for concrete, timber poles for concrete falsework are normally provided by the villagers themselves either in the form of voluntary labour for winning stone and aggregates or as a contribution from the village of a portion of their timber resources. As in the case of the voluntary labour similar incentive considerations apply.

Imported materials such as reinforcing steel and nationally indigenous materials such as cement and sawn timber are provided by the RDD. When planning the road the designs adopted deliberately minimise the requirement for materials which are not available locally. Thus for retaining walls dry random rubble would be used in preference to random rubble in cement mortar even when the value of the labour and materials in the former would exceed the latter. The greater the proportion of the resource inputs provided by the village itself the greater the sense that the road is *their* road.

The construction methods are entirely labour based. The only equipment which might be provided consists of:
a) pumps for dewatering structural foundations;
b) dump trucks where materials have to be moved beyond the range of hand carry or donkey transport;
c) concrete mixers — only in the case of large reinforced concrete structures (only two mixers are available for more than 90 projects):
d) concrete poker-type vibrators (the RDD's total holding is 3 units).

It might be considered that the use of voluntary labour as a construction resource would divert labour from agricultural production activities. In fact there is a considerable reservoir of unemployed and underemployed labour available in the villages on a seasonal basis.

## 4. Design criteria

The design criteria must always be considered as being flexible. They must also be compatible with the resources available and the construction techniques to be used. The design criteria discussed below are orientated to a situation of voluntary or semi-voluntary labour-based construction using the minimum of manufactured materials.

The use of unskilled village labour which works only on one project does not allow the building up of elementary construction skills in the labour force. The construction techniques involved must therefore be confined to very basic unskilled operations plus the use of any indigenous skill available in the local environment such as dry-stone masonry, construction of earth and stone coffer dams, etc. Designs have been deliberately developed which can tolerate such limitations in the resources available. This has led to the extensive use of random rubble masonry (both dry and in cement mortar), crib construction and gabion construction.

There is a further constraint to be considered when designing roads which are constructed by voluntary labour. The villagers will only do such work as they consider necessary to achieve the objective, i.e. a means of access to their village. Thus, if they consider that a 3.5 m or 4 m wide formation width is adequate it is most difficult to get them to construct the 6 m wide formation which might be dictated by considerations of traffic use and safety. Similarly if they do not consider a culvert to be necessary they will not construct it. In this type of work therefore design criteria must always be considered as guideline targets rather than an immutable minimum.

The design criteria adopted for tertiary roads in Afghanistan are based on the following assumptions:
- a) that the Average Daily Traffic (ADT) does not exceed 100 vehicles per day (vpd);
- b) that the traffic mix will be in the proportions of 17 per cent cars and jeeps, 33 per cent light trucks and buses (1½ tonne payload or 20 seats) and 50 per cent medium trucks and buses (6 tonne payload or 40 seats);
- c) that traffic delays up to 24 hours are acceptable.

The rural tertiary road design standards in use are given in Annex 1 at the end of this chapter.

Various types of structure are now in use. Most of these

make maximum use of local materials. In the case of bridges, for instance, timber trusses up to 30 metre spans have been designed. In the case of culverts, the usual type used up to the present time has random rubble masonry walls with reinforced concrete slab decks. Pipe culverts are seldom used because of the constraints of casting the pipes on the sites with the lack of control over concrete quality. Transport problems preclude the use of pipes manufactured at central locations.

Retaining walls and bank protection are generally of random rubble dry-stone masonry. The village people have developed skills in its use as it is used for boundary walling, housing and land terrace wallings. Such walling is often "stitched" with brushwood or timber poles.

Caseways or "saddle" bridges have often been adopted because in Afghanistan's semi-arid climate there are a large number of stream and river crossings which are dry (or have very small flows) for the greater part of the year. Such drainage channels are called washes. At certain times, often for very short periods, such washes run with considerable flows. They are often very wide (up to 1 km) and to bridge them with a dry crossing for tertiary road traffic volumes would be uneconomic. In some cases the flow pattern is such that for nine months of the year the flow will be nil or minimal followed by three months of significant flow interspersed with periods of high flow of very short duration. The solution adopted for this situation is to construct a causeway which has a cross section designed to discharge the three months significant flow at a fordable depth (usually taken as 35 cms) allowing the road to be interrupted during the short periods of high flow. Such causeways may be of unvented masonry or pervious gabion construction. In cases where there is a significant dry-weather flow, slab culvert vents are provided.

The roads constructed by RDD are not normally paved, consisting of earth or improved earth surfaces. In the rare cases where gravel surfacing is provided it is usually spread in a number of thin layers, each layer being compacted by traffic. No compaction equipment is owned or used by RDD. Compaction of embankments and behind abutments of bridges and culverts is achieved by the use of wooden-pole rammers. Action is being taken to acquire a limited number of vibrating rollers and impact rammers to improve compaction in such cases.

## 5. Stage design for roads

The concept of stage construction of roads is well-known. It consists of the construction of the various elements of a road, earthwork, sub-base, base and surfacing in stages. Each stage is constructed at the point in time when traffic volumes dictate that particular stage. Thus, in the first instance, when low-traffic volumes are forecast, the road is constructed with narrower formation widths and lower pavement strengths than are predicted for the final stage.

In such cases it has usually been assumed that the road must be constructed on the same horizontal alignment in the first stage as will be required in the final stage. The vertical centre line may be adjusted in stages to accommodate the progressively higher sight distance standards demanded by increasing traffic volume. The same may apply to the widening of cuts or removal of obstacles to increase horizontal sight distances. The horizontal alignment of the centre line, apart from minor adjustments such as the insertion of transition curves and adjustments to curve radii within the earthwork width, is however usually fixed by considerations of the final traffic volume to be accommodated.

This general method of stage construction is a valid and economic concept in flat or rolling country as the effect of higher horizontal alignment standards involves a comparatively small increment in earthwork costs. For example, the cost differential of joining tangents by large radius curves instead of small radius curves is usually a small percentage of the total earthwork cost. In mountainous country however, where a road is running up a steep-sided valley (a very prevalent case) the cost differentials may be very high. If a large number of small radius curves are acceptable the road centre line can follow the contour with a minimum of earthwork. A higher standard of curvature and sight distance will involve cutting through spurs and filling through re-entrants. This not only involves higher volumes of earthwork but also the longitudinal movement of earth from cut to fill as opposed to the lower, standard case of lateral movement of earth short distances from cut to downhill waste. In addition, the filling of re-entrants on steep-side slopes often means considerable expenditure on retaining walls and pre-fill benching.

In such cases the principle of stage design can often achieve significant savings on initial construction costs. There is no doubt that such an approach will result in a higher total construction investment by the time the final stage is reached. However, if the traffic growth rate is expected to be small and the initial traffic volume is low (less than 50 vpd) the effect of postponing the capital expenditure required by the later stages can, by the effect of discounting the costs, result in lower net present costs. This effect, in cases where benefits are low, can have a decisive effect on the economic equation and convert a non-viable to a viable investment.

The question of ruling and maximum gradients, which are often critical design parameters in mountainous regions, requires special attention if stage design is to be adopted. The gradient criteria should be applied to the *final improved alignment* and the profile of the initial alignment adjusted to control points where the initial alignment crosses the final alignment. Thus the distance along the centre lines between two coincidental points on the two alignments might be 1,000 metres on the initial alignment and 500 metres on the final alignment. If the final design grade were to be 5 per cent, i.e. a rise of 25 metres over the 500 metres section then the gradient on the initial design section would have to be restricted to 2.5 per cent so that when the final design is achieved the final design gradient criteria can be met.

A second point requiring careful planning is the question of culverts and drainage structures. In the initial stage permanent culverts should only be located in positions where the initial and final alignments coincide or nearly coincide. In other cases either road dips (pitched to prevent erosion) can be provided, or dry-stone random rubble abutment walls supporting precast concrete slabs should be used. At the final stage these can be transferred to the final location culverts.

Bridges should be considered as control or obligatory points and constructed on the final alignment. In cases where this proves very difficult to achieve, prefabricated bridges such as Bailey can be used. Alternatively where traffic growth indicates that the final alignment will not be required within the life span of a temporary bridge (say 15-20 years) then a timber structure can be provided. In cases where initial traffic volumes are low (say less than 25 vpd) interruption of traffic for limited periods (say 24-48 hours) can usually be accepted and pitched fords can be constructed on the initial alignment.

The decision to adopt stage design must be preceded by a carefully considered judgement of the traffic growth pattern (an analysis based on statistical method is seldom possible). An element of risk is of course always involved but the possible savings offered by the method are such that they allow much needed access to be provided to villages and small towns which would otherwise remain in isolation with all that involves in terms of the lack of economic and social development.

This approach can also offer a solution to the dilemma of being unable to construct a road to the final alignment requirements because its construction would require mechanical equipment (heavy rock cuts, etc.) which is not available in the country. The stage design approach enables a road to be built, as the side hill cut operation can always be achieved by hand labour using handtools. Thus, road access can be provided in many cases where the conventional design approach would involve costs which rule out viability. In such cases the villages and towns involved are condemned to indefinite stagnation in an isolated environment.

## 6. **Organisation and management of labour**

There are four distinct elements in the process of converting human physical energy into infrastructure. These are:
   a) the generation and maintenance of the energy output itself;
   b) the acquisition and application of skill;
   c) the identification and provision of optimum tools and equipment to provide the means of converting the energy and the skill into physical infrastructure;
   d) the organisation and methods used in the construction process to co-ordinate the three elements (a), (b) and (c).

In the normal case the maintenance of output is a function of incentives. The incentive may be financial reward or it may be by the negative incentive of a closely supervised environment which insists on a certain minimum output as a requirement of employment. Financial incentives may be on an individual or on a group/gang basis. Such incentives include piecework where payment is in direct proportion to production and task plus bonus systems where a minimum task is linked to a day's work and additional payment is made for each unit of production achieved in addition to the minimum task. In some cases a mixture of the financial incentive and supervision incentive systems operates when labour contractors are employed[1], the contractor being paid on a production basis and his labour being paid on a supervised fixed-wage basis. But such systems are not considered desirable as they lead to the exploitation of labour by labour contractors.

In the case of purely voluntary labour the incentive, while it has an individual element, is essentially a group incentive and not directly linked to financial reward. As the labour is voluntary the relationship between the supervisor and the labour is quite different than that between a normal employer and employee. In the case of voluntary labour it is absolutely essential that the supervisory personnel adopt an attitude of offering their services to the village to assist them in achieving their objective. In the case of structures the fact that RDD provides cement and reinforcement provides some hold over the village but in the case of roads the provision of such materials is often minimal and control over the construction must be achieved by the co-operative attitude and leadership qualities of the RDD personnel.

The case where voluntary labour is supported by WFP aid lies between the purely voluntary case and the normal case. However the Afghan farmer is a fiercely independent individualist and the methods of man management adopted must tend towards the voluntary-labour case rather than the employed-labour case.

There are certain construction or quasi-construction skills which are inherent in Afghan village life. These vary somewhat in differing areas of the country in sympathy with the locally available construction materials. One skill which is very widespread is the management of flowing water. Irrigation is the life-blood of the Afghan farmer and he is highly skilled in drainage works, the construction of coffer and diversion dams. In areas where stone is available, masonry skills both in dry-stone walling and mud-mortar walling are indigenous. Labour which works on construction projects on a continuous basis although nominally unskilled, has in fact significant skills both in excavation work and in support of skilled artisans. Such labour also has an awareness of the construction site environment with its attendant hazards. The acquisition of these skills is usually by a process of absorption through working with experienced construction labour. In the case of construction labour which is voluntarily supplied by a village for an isolated project the construction operation is a new experience and there is no core of experienced labour to emulate. This labour has to be trained in organisation methods and safety precautions completely from scratch by the RDD supervisory personnel. This process has to be repeated for every job because in every new project the labour, being indigenous to the village concerned, starts with no construction experience.

Before the construction team arrives on the site a construction plan has been prepared at RDD headquarters which shows in bar-chart form the starting date and time programmed for each operation and also the resource inputs required. Earthwork on roads is often carried on at several locations at the same time. These locations are selected on the basis of convenient distances from individual villages. Having identified the sections of road and the quantity of labour to be provided by the village or villages assigned to that section, the technician meets the Malik (headman) of the village and discusses the construction of the section in detail. The work is set out and the shape of the excavation is shown to the villagers. Work then proceeds supervised by the construction supervisors who indicate lines and levels and advise on management at the site to achieve the optimum productivity. This advice covers such points as the best division of labour between excavators, carriers, placers in fill or throwers to spoil. As has been stated previously the productivity of purely voluntary labour is a direct function of their own motivation and site management is largely confined to showing the labour how they can achieve greater productivity with the same effort.

In the case of labour supported by WFP food rations, reward (in terms of food rations) can be correlated with productivity. Production norms have been established for excavation tasks. These norms have been based on six soil categories linked to the process of excavation (table 1).

Table 1: Man-hours of labour-required per cubic metre

| | Soil type[1] | | | | | |
|---|---|---|---|---|---|---|
| | 1 | 2 | 3 | 4 | 5 | 6 |
| Excavate into barrows or baskets | 1.0 | 1.6 | 2.0 | 3.0 | 6.0 | 10.0 |
| Excavate into trucks | 1.6 | 2.2 | 2.8 | 3.6 | 6.6 | 10.8 |
| Trench excavation 1.5 metres | 2.0 | 3.6 | 4.0 | 5.0 | 10.0 | 14.0 |
| Hauling in barrows over 20 metres | 1.0 | 1.1 | 1.2 | 1.3 | 1.4 | 1.4 |
| Hauling by baskets over 20 metres | 1.8 | 1.9 | 1.9 | 2.1 | 2.5 | 2.5 |
| Spreading and compacting in 15-cm layers | 1.0 | 1.0 | n.a. | 1.0 | n.a. | n.a. |

[1] Soil type  1 — Loose sand or soil
2 — firm sand or soil
3 — clay or heavy adhesive soil
4 — compact soil or gravel
5 — soft rock
6 — hard rock

These norms are translated into metre-runs of completed road for the various configurations in the section being constructed. These configurations normally fall into four general categories:

A. Flat ground, no embankments. Side drains excavated and filled to centre to form camber. 5.50 m wide between drains.

B. Embankment 1 m high, 6 m wide.

C. Side hill cut on side slopes up to 30°.

D. Side hill cut on side slopes over 30°.

The quantity of excavation, carry, and filling in each metre-run is calculated for the average section and the number of man-hours work involved. This is translated into rations of food on the basis of eight hours work. The number of rations allowed per metre-run for each length of each configuration in the section is then agreed with the labour force. The section is then divided into "lengths" with an approximately equal number of rations payable for each length. Each length is marked and allocated to a group of labour (a gang). Payment of rations is made on production achieved. In cases where the food ration is supplemented by a cash payment the cash payment is made on an individual man-day basis rather than on a productivity basis. This is done to comply with government accounting regulations.

Skilled labour employed on the construction of bridges, culverts, retaining walls and drainage outfalls is paid on a man-day basis. WFP-supported unskilled labour is paid food rations at the rate of one ration per man-day worked.

7. **Methods, tools and equipment**
The greatest bulk of the work performed is in excavation which is carried out entirely by hand (including rock drilling). The tools used are:
    a) long-handled, round-mouthed shovels;
    b) picks with sharp and chisel points;
    c) crowbars with moil points for soft rock and boulder excavation and with chisel points for rock drilling;
    d) two-man carrying litters.

These tools are the traditional tools of the farming community of Afghanistan.

The bulk of excavation in road works is in side hill cut or in the excavation of parallel drains on level ground using the material excavated from the drains to form a central camber. Movement of material from the excavation to spoil rarely exceeds 10 m and is usually of the order of 5 to 6 m. In the case of side hill cut excavated material is moved laterally to waste down the hillside. This is achieved by double handling the material, the excavator throwing to the excavated bench and a second man throwing it to waste by shovel. The number of excavators served by one double handler depends on the soil category involved and the length of throw. In the case of soil category 4 (see section 6, seventh paragraph) which forms a large proportion of the excavated material, one double handler can serve two or three excavators. If the distance to be moved is more than 6 m (two throws, triple handled) carrying litters may be employed. Attempts have been made to introduce wheelbarrows as these have about half the labour input of a two-man litter. These efforts have had mixed success but where sufficient barrows can be obtained of suitable quality the indications are that they will be accepted in most cases. The use of baskets, headpans, etc., is not accepted by the Afghan farmer who is not accustomed to carrying any load on the head. Where carries exceed about 30 m, donkeys with twin panniers are used if they are available and can be spared from other transport demands. In cases where there are other competitive transport demands at the time of construction (e.g. taking the surplus crops to the bazaar), donkey transport has to be hired, at other times it is provided free by the village. In cases where long carries (in excess of 1 km) are involved the RDD provides dump trucks. These cases are usually confined to hauling construction materials such as masonry stone and concrete aggregates rather than excavated material to fill or spoil.

Rock drilling is done with crowbars which are "jumped" in the hole (not driven by hammer). A group of three men are usually employed. Two men "jump" the bar and the third washes and clears drillings from the hole, a length of hooked wire being used for this purpose. The bars are usually 1½ m long and 40-50 mm in diameter. Productivity achieved depends on the rock type but rarely exceeds 1 m per shift. It is therefore a slow and laborious process which often holds up other work. The RDD is procuring self-contained mechanical drills to speed up the process. Due to access difficulties the use of air-compressors and jack-hammers will be confined to sites where truck access is possible.

The greatest problems are encountered when excavating in pits or trenches for foundations, particularly to bridge piers and abutments where dewatering is necessary. The normal method is to construct a coffer dam or diversion dam of mud and stones reinforced with brushwood. The excavation is carried out in open pits without timbering which means that, allowing for tolerable side slopes, the area of the excavation is large. In gravel and boulder beds where percolation rates are high the volume of water entering the excavation is very high and when heads of more than about 2 m are involvd the inflow becomes unmanageable. 10 cm and 15 cm suction centrifugal pumps are used but in practice it has been found that foundation

depths beyond about 2 m are extremely difficult to achieve in the dry. This is being tackled in a number of ways:
 a) by modifying designs by adopting shallow self-scour protecting structures (gabion and cribs);
 b) by modifying designs by adopting open caissons to reduce foundation areas and reduce inflows;
 c) to acquire excavation equipment (back hoes);
 d  to introduce timbering techniques.

It is difficult to introduce new tools and techniques to the extremely conservative Afghan farmer. This is particularly the case where voluntary labour is involved. The farmer will do it his way or not at all. It requires great persistence and the clear demonstration that a method is easier if there is to be any chance of getting it adopted. Construction supervisors and field engineers and technicians continuously try to improve techniques but the process is slow. A second problem when the labour force continuously changes from village to village is that by the time one village is convinced that a new technique is worth while a new batch of villagers from another village takes over the construction process.

## 8. Special considerations involved in the use of voluntary village labour

The primary objective of the Rural Development Department is to raise the standard of living of the rural people of Afghanistan by providing such supplementary inputs to the efforts of the people themselves as will help them to greater efficiency, productivity and social well-being. In the context of road building, it is not RDD's primary objective to construct the roads themselves but to use the road-building process as a vehicle for enhancing the self-reliance of the villages concerned and to increase their capacity to manage their own resources for the benefit of the community.

This policy of giving primary importance to voluntary village participation poses a number of problems which are not generally encountered when planning comes from the top downwards and construction is by paid labour.

The tertiary road construction programme emerges from the aggregation of village requests to construct roads and their agreement to provide the labour to do so. The shape of the programme and the relative economic priorities of the projects comprising the programme are not therefore based on rational over-all regional requirements. When the RDD receives a request from a village to build a road a socio-economic survey is carried out which examines the transport need and makes a rough comparison between benefits (both quantifiable and non-quantifiable) and costs. The voluntary labour and local materials contribution is not counted in these costs as they are not transferable to other alternative projects. If this survey demonstrates viability the project is normally approved. When considering viability in this context the position of the road vis-a-vis the rest of the road system of the region is considered and a project would be approved provided it contributed to the totality of the transport system. However it might not, as an individual road, make a higher contribution than any other alternative. In this sense therefore it would offend against the principles of rational planning that investments should be progressively made in those projects giving the highest return. The attitude adopted by the RDD is therefore dictated by their basic policy of bottom-up initiative and not by the strict rationale of economic planning criteria.

Typical costs of tertiary roads in Afghanistan range from $1,500 per km for roads with few structures and no major bridges, to $12,000 per km for roads in isolated mountainous areas involving paid labour and considerable structural work in retaining walls, culverts and bridges. These costs demonstrate the simple design criteria adopted.

Design criteria which are based on good technical practice and considerations of functional efficiency and safety are not always self-evident requirements to a village which is required to make major contributions to a scheme. For example, a road is now under construction to link the Parsa valley to the main road in the province of Parwan bordering Central Afghanistan. This road is entirely in side hill cut through difficult boulder-strewn soil, rock talus slopes and, in some lengths, solid rock. Excavation conditions are difficult and laborious. The design criteria call for a cut bench width of 6 m, 5.50 m for the formation and 0.50 m for the hillside drain. The villagers have excavated a bench 3.5-4.0 m in width and light buses are negotiating the road and providing a transport service. The villagers are most reluctant to provide any further labour to widen this bench to the design width and it may prove impossible to achieve the design criteria. The village has achieved its objective, a transport connection which is operating. As far as they are concerned this is enough. On this same road there is a difficult climbing section involving a double hair-pin bend. Drystone walling has been built to provide the bare minimum geometry which will enable a light truck to negotiate the bend by reversing on the hair-pin bends. This is a dangerous procedure and from a highway engineering point of view the design is unacceptable. A new design has been prepared which will require new retaining walls to be constructed. The first reactions of the villagers to providing labour to construct these walls was unfavourable but it is hoped that they will be persuaded to construct the new design before a major accident occurs.

Labour management has to be based on persuasion and mutual respect between the RDD team and the village. It cannot be based on the usual criteria of labour discipline and financial incentive. The incentives and motivation behind the village's voluntary contribution are discussed in section 3 (paragraphs 1-4). This requires an entirely different style of management based on leadership and sympathy rather than "commercial" methods. Arising from this is the fact that the construction processes involved have to be discussed in much greater detail to convince the villagers that the method advocated is to their advantage.

The present policy of initiation, planning and execution of tertiary road projects from the bottom up and with the close involvement of the village at all stages will be continued. As virtually the whole of village contributions consist of unskilled labour the use of this resource is obligatory which in turn means that labour-based methods must continue to be used. This policy is not confined to road construction but extends to all infrastructure works carried out by the Rural Development Department.

**Notes and references**

[1] Editor's note: the use of labour contractors is not encouraged by the ILO as it often leads to abuse. Their use is covered by the Convention concerning the protection of wages, Convention No. 95, adopted by the International Labour Conference in September 1952.

## Annex I — Tertiary road design standards

a) formation width:
   i) in cut 5.50 m excluding drains;
   ii) in fill 6.00 m;
   iii) in rock 3.50 m excluding drains;
b) carriageway width 3.50 m;
c) passing places:
   i) generally 6.50 m wide, 35 m long at intervals of 500 m or the sight distance whichever is the less;
   ii) in rock cuts 5.50 m wide 25 m long at intervals of 150 m;
d) gradients:
   i) over-all gradients: earth surfaced 3 per cent, gravel surfaced 4 per cent;
   ii) maximum gradients: earth surfaced 10 per cent, gravel surfaced 12 per cent.
   Gradients through sharp bends, particularly hairpin bends, should not exceed 5 per cent between the tangent points of the bend plus 15 m at each end;
e) curvature: the maximum radii compatible with the terrain should be adopted with the following minima:
   i) minimum inside radius of carriageway — 9 m;
   ii) minimum outside radius of carriageway — 13.5 m;
f) surfacing:
   i) generally gravel surfacing will only be provided when traffic exceeds 100 pcu per day (cars 1 pcu, light trucks 1 1/2 pcu, medium trucks 3 pcu);
   ii) gravel surfacing will also be provided in particular cases where soil moisture or drainage conditions make it necessary;
   iii) in cases where the natural earth is of a plastic nature, cohesionless material such as sand or fine gravel is mixed with the top of the formation to stabilise the surface;
   iv) in other cases the natural formation will be used.

# CHAPTER 8. THE BORDER ROADS ORGANISATION IN INDIA: LABOUR-INTENSIVE CONSTRUCTION ON A LARGE SCALE

*by Major General J.S. Soin*
*Director, Border Roads Organisation*

## 1. Introduction

The Border Roads Organisation (BRO) was created in 1960 to undertake road construction programmes in North and North-East India in areas where little or no road existed. The urgency for socio-economic development of these backward areas and the impediments to achieving this owing to the lack of road communications resulted in a crash programme of priority roads being roughly assesed in 1960 and efforts made to mobilise resources. The programme of road construction envisaged in the formative stages of the organisation was the completion of about 3,000 kms of roads (new construction and improvement) over a three-year period.

It was expected that when the objectives of the crash programme were realised, it would be possible for other development agencies to carry out maintenance and improvements and to expand the road communication complexes with many more arterial routes and feeder roads in the years ahead. However, the need for faster and dependable road communications systems increased and the BRO was entrusted with the construction of more roads on the basis of their performance and expertise.

## 2. Terrain and climate — effect on technology, design and specification

The BRO had to undertake work in areas of difficult terrain and extreme climatic conditions. The terrain is mostly mountainous, with many escarpments where the strata is geologically very young, and unstable. The roads have been constructed from the foothills going up to 5,000 metres altitude.

There are regions which are generally arid and experience heavy snowfalls during winter months, and where very low temperatures obtain, in certain places as low as -40°C with high velocity winds as well. In other regions, forest growth is dense and rainfall is as high as 500 cms per year with frequent high-intensity rainfall during short periods, often associated with cloudbursts. Severe weather conditions pertain for almost five to six months of the year.

These climatic conditions obviously have an adverse effect on the efficiency of workmen and on the performance of machines and materials. Terrain and climatic conditions have, therefore, a special significance and have long-term effects on the organisational set-up, the design and specifications for the roads, the type of technology and the mode of working.

Initially, the bad terrain and extreme climatic conditions were governing factors in the adoption of machine-intensive work on roads. Availability of labour was also found to be poor as the working conditions were not conducive to attract people to venture into such areas. However, with the opening up of the areas and development taking place these areas became more habitable and working conditions improved so that it was possible to make a beneficial transition towards more labour-intensive methods.

## 3. **Design standards**

The width of roads constructed was that considered adequate to allow free one-way traffic or restricted two-way traffic. While adopting these specifications, it has also been kept in view that it will be possible to upgrade the roads if such a necessity arises due to traffic growth. A ruling gradient of 1 in 20 for hill roads was fixed keeping in view the effect of altitude and snowfall on vehicles.

To make the best use of local materials and those produced during the course of earthwork such as trees, stones and so on, it was decided at the start to provide temporary log culverts, retaining and drainage structures with stone masonry (wherever possible with dry stone), to use stone as soling to form the sub-base of the pavements, to limit paved roads to 3.75 metres and adopt a simple type of wearing course, like surface dressing, for the pavement. Even in the construction of bridges for spanning small streams and major rivers, prefabricated equipment components were accepted, to be replaced with permanent bridges later on.

## 4. Selection of technology

The road construction programmes entrusted to the BRO were very large and were required in a relatively short period.

It became clear that the appropriate technology for road construction would be a combination of equipment-intensive and labour-based methods. This principle has been quite successfully adopted by the BRO not only in respect of road construction but for maintenance as well.

### 4.1 *Balancing of machines and labour: new construction*

For reasons outlined previously, it was initially planned to make the BRO basically machine based. However there was a considerable gap between the availability and requirements of machines necessary to realise the stated targets. In order to make up these shortfalls by manual efforts, it was necessary to evaluated the relative effects of using manpower as against machines and to examine the extent to which the labour-based methods could be used in realising the targets without in any way increasing the fixed and predetermined overhead costs. Accordingly, the BRO carried out a study of the labour required to replace machines for the major items of works in road building, namely earthwork in road formation, protective works and pavement construction. The results of the study are summarised below:

a) *Number of men required to replace equipment*
  i) Crawler tractor   : 200 men
     (150-180 hp)
  ii) Compressor       : 170 men
  iii) Stone crusher   : 100 men
     (5-6 tons/hour)

b) *The number of men required for 100 kms of road length per year even if earthwork and surfacing is done by equipment*
  i) Earthwork    : 3,000 men per day (jungle clearance, dressing of hill slopes, assisting machines, levelling road formation and so on)

ii) Protective and
drainage works : 1,300 men (all works) per day
iii) Pavement : 1,900 men (stone collection, feeding of crushers, spreading of various courses, watering, assisting road rollers, berm dressing and so on)
Total : 6,200 men per day

c) The required labour force to execute 100 kms of road construction by various percentages of machines and labour (assuming that protective works have to be done only by labour) is depicted in Figure 1 overleaf.

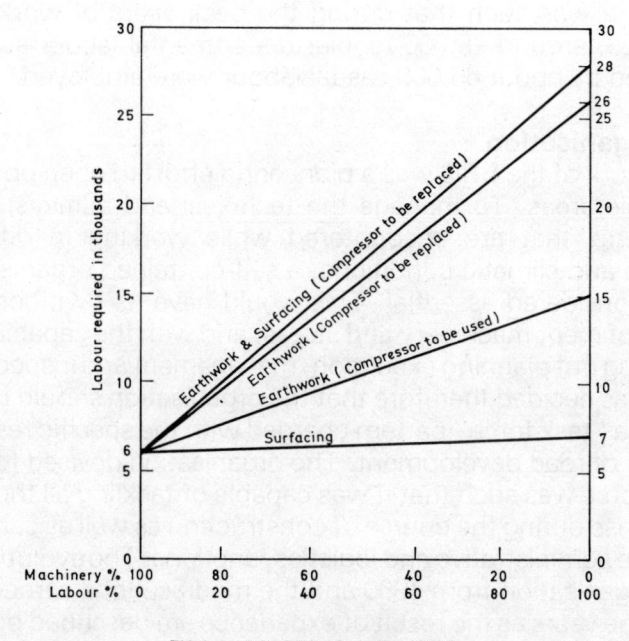

FIG.1 MACHINERY AGAINST LABOUR

d) It will be seen from Figure 1 that the labour requirement steadily increases with the reduction in the proportion of machines. According to the graph the annual requirement of labour for executing 400 kms of road works per year is of the order of 25,000 men if equipment-intensive methods are used.

The use of a large labour force for road works poses recruitment problems which imply increases in the number of supervisory and administrative staff. Resorting to man-intensive earthwork has its own drawbacks and the deployment of men over virgin stretches of land becomes difficult. Further, wide variations in the requirements for labour will create problems at both the recruitment and discharge stages. The most important factor that has a bearing on costs is the requirement to accelerate road formation works. If this is not done the provision of the surfacing and protective works is delayed and causes an escalation of direct and indirect costs.

Nevertheless the move to a more labour-based method of working was such that during the peak years of work, i.e. 1965-68, around 25,000 regular departmental labour supplemented by about 65,000 casual labour were employed.

## 5. Organisation

The work of the BRO was a pioneering effort to open up inaccessible areas. To manage the technical and administrative problems that are encountered while working in difficult terrain and climatic conditions, a self-contained organisation was considered essential. This would have its own complement of men, machinery and stores, and with the capability of carrying out planning execution, management and inspection.

It was decided therefore that the organisation should be set up on a "task force" pattern charged with the specific responsibility of road development. The organisation devised for the task force was such that it was capable of tackling all the jobs that arise during the course of construction as well as carrying out the administrative and logistics functions. The evolution of the organisation from 1960 and the modifications carried out over the years as the result of experience are described below.

The task force, headed by a superintending engineer, was charged with the responsibility of technical and financial control over the constructional activities. The task force was given three types of *unit* to enable it to discharge its functions:

    a) construction units;
    b) logistic units;
    c) administrative units.

Construction units are allotted to task forces for the following purposes:

a) construction company in charge of a sector of road;
b) earth-moving plant company holding a complement of tractors for earthwork. This provides the plant needs of the construction company;
c) construction equipment company for holding equipment like compressors, rock drills, stone crushers, concrete mixers, and so on, to be used by the construction company;
d) pioneer company to provide department (regular) labour force.

To assist the construction companies in their tasks, the following supporting units were provided:
a) field workshop to provide repair and maintenance facilities for vehicles, plant and equipment;
b) transport company/transport platoons to supply vehicles for construction and administrative purposes.

To provide administrative services, the following units were constituted:
a) supply platoons to provide rations and primary and secondary oils;
b) workshop and park company to hold and supply stores;
c) medical units;
d) postal sections.

All the units indicated above were placed under the task force which controlled the ground organisation and whose functions were technical, financial and administrative. The task force normally had two or three construction companies and one each of the supporting and administrative units and two pioneer companies. Each of the task forces were capable of being employed at any time on about 100 kms of new roads in different stages of development.

A task force with the organisational structure described was found to be effective in the formative stages. However, in due course of time, with the progressive improvement of communications and the necessity to adopt superior specifications including provision of large-scale protective work and all-weather pavement, it was found necessary to reorganise some of the units on a functional basis.

Therefore, a review of the functioning of the units of the BRO was carried out.

The review resulted in the following types of unit under the task force:
a) road construction company;
b) road maintenance platoon;
c) surfacing platoon;
d) permanent works platoon;
e) formation cutting platoon;
f) transport platoon.

The expected output of the functional platoons is as follows:
a) formation cutting platoon: 20 kms of road per year;
b) permanent works platoon: 300,000 dollars per year;
c) surfacing platoon: 20 kms of pavement per year;
d) road maintenance platoon: 100 kms road maintenance; 25 kms of renewal of wearing course and 80,000 dollars of protective works.

Each task force may have two to four road construction companies. Each road construction company may have either two formation cutting platoons or three surfacing/permanent works platoons or five road maintenance platoons with a budget of 1 million dollars per year. As such, a task force has the potential to undertake works worth 3 million dollars per year.

Such an organisation has been found to function effectively. The controlling headquarters for this organisation is that of the chief engineers of projects who each have two to four task forces under them. The project chief engineer has over-all responsibility for the task forces under him and his jurisdiction is defined from work and geographical considerations. The chief engineer is responsible to ensure the arrangement of all resources as well as their management and personnel administration.

The projects come under the over-all control of the Director-General, Border Roads who is responsible for co-ordinating the functions of the organisation, laying down technical standards, procurement of vehicles, plant and equipment as well as the allocation of resources and funds to projects.

For the construction of 100 kms of new road in one year the rough requirement for the major categories of personnel and machinery is tabulated below:

| Category | Requirement |
|---|---|
| *Manpower* | |
| 1 Officers (engineers) | 100 |
| 2 Supervisors | |
| (a) senior | 200 |
| (b) junior | 250 |
| 3 Tradesmen: (masons, concretors and so on) | 750 |
| 4 Operators and mechanics | 1 000 |
| 5 Regular labour | 3 000 |
| 6 Casual labour (skilled and unskilled) | 9 000 |
| *Machinery* | |
| 1 Light vehicles | 100 |
| 2 Load carriers (3 to 7 tons) | 350 |
| 3 Crawler tractors (150-180 hp) | 45 |
| 4 Compressors (2 drills) | 45 |
| 5 Road rollers | 25 |
| 6 Stone crushers up to 10 t/hour | 20 |
| 7 Bitumen heaters | 15 |
| 8 Hot-mix plant (20-30 t/hour) | 3 |
| 9 Concrete mixers (up to 0.3m$^3$) | 6 |

## 6. **Employment of labour**

### 6.1 *Departmental (regular) labour*

Both skilled and unskilled labour is employed on road works. The BRO has a certain complement of these in its own establishment who are regular government employees paid according to fixed scales of pay. Certain special concessions like rations, clothing and so on are also provided. There are some 3,000 skilled and 20,000 unskilled workers in this category. They are moved from place to place as necessary. Their cost to the BRO is about twice that of casual labour.

### 6.2 *Casual labour*

In many instances the BRO has supplemented departmental (regular) labour with a large complement of civil labour recruited locally or from outside and introduced into the area. Civil labour is employed on monthly rates of pay but they are not regular government employees and do not have any permanent hold on their job. Their services are liable for termination at any time and are governed by normal labour laws.

Imported labour is recruited from outside the immediate project area when there is scarcity of local labour. They are

recruited for a minimum period of six months and are paid train/bus fares to the project site from the place of recruitment and some pocket expenses. The facilities provided to the casual labour both local and imported are as follow:
   a) issue of ration on payment;
   b) limited medical services;
   c) weekly paid holidays;
   d) improvised living accommodation;
   e) death/injury compensation.

The wages fixed for civil labour are not less than those for similar categories employed in other government agencies in the area, and also take into account the difficult working conditions where they are deployed. The range of rates prevalent are:
   a) unskilled: 20-25 dollars per month;
   b) skilled: 25-30 dollars per month.

The availability of labour is seasonal as labour is mainly drawn from rural areas and they go in search of employment during the non-agriculture season. By and large, the BRO has been able to get an assured supply of labour because gangs or groups of labour have been working for years with particular units. Thus, they have moved with the units wherever new works are taken up: moreover labour has taken up permanent residence in many of the areas where road communications have been developed and are employed as maintenance gangs.

The average strength of skilled and unskilled casual labour employed by the BRO over the last few years is 3,000 skilled and 60,000 unskilled.

## 7. Contracts

The bulk of the work of the BRO is done departmentally. However, with the opening up of the areas, the availability of construction contractors, as well as contractors for transport, has increased considerably. In view of this, it was considered desirable to entrust some works on contract, at least in the areas where development has taken place. Accordingly, certain works like supply and transportation of stone, aggregates, sand and so on, and to a limited extent construction of small items of work like culverts and retaining walls, are being awarded to contractors to augment departmental resources especially vehicles. In addition, the construction of major bridges is being entrusted to specialist firms.

## 8. Logistics

One of the major problems of the BRO when operating in remote and difficult areas is logistics. It involves not only procurement and provisioning of an assortment of vehicles, plant and equipment and other stores but also transportation to work sites situated as much as 500-600 kms away from railheads.

Enormous efforts are required to position all types of stores and vehicles, plant and equipment at work sites at proper times and in predetermined quantities. These should be available in a state of fitness for utilisation. Unless the logistics problems are tackled, the constrcution work will not proceed as programmed.

One of the responsibilities of the Director-General, Border Roads and Project Chief Engineer is to look into the aspects of logistics and inventory management. Base workshops cater for repairs of vehicles, plant and equipment and provide a spares back-up. Stock and inventory control functions for constructional stores are attended to by stores depots under the project chief engineers.

## 9. Conclusions

Developing countries embarking on road construction programmes have to choose between labour-based and capital-intensive methods keeping in view the problems obtaining in their countries. It is possible to undertake large-scale construction programmes by organising the construction force modelled on the lines of the BRO.

The BRO has moved steadily over the years from a reliance on equipment-intensive methods to the use of effective labour-based methods.

It should be borne in mind however that the BRO is run along military lines. Whilst this produces relative efficiency it is not necessarily representative of labour-based work throughout India. It does indicate however that even when large numbers of unskilled labour are employed it is possible to organise and manage labour-based methods effectively.

## CHAPTER 9. SOCIAL AND ENVIRONMENTAL FACTORS: LESSONS FROM IRAN

*by R.S. McCutcheon*

### 1. Introduction[1]

Several innovatory rural development programmes have recently been initiated in Iran. One of these — the Selseleh Integrated Development Project (SIDP)[2] is based in the Alashtar Valley of the Lorestan Province, about 450 kms south of Tehran. The town of Alashtar has a population of 6,000 inhabitants and is the commercial and administrative centre of a fertile and well-watered plain, which has over 200 villages whose total population is about 40,000. The people of the plain are members of the Lur Tribe, partly settled and partly nomadic. The income of the region derives almost entirely from nomadic pastoralism and agriculture, the main cash crops being wheat, soy beans and sugarbeet.

The SIDP was based upon notions of self-reliance and participation. Particular stress was laid upon the need for both collective and individual development to be endogenous (i.e. to grow from within the local society itself) and not be based upon alien models. Trainees were to be selected from among the local population. At the end of their training programme it was intended that they should return to their villages and act as "agents of change". The trainees would help the people decide upon their own developmental priorities. Concurrent with the training programmes it was intended that the project should initiate the provision of a developmental infrastructure (public baths, schools, roads, etc.) in accordance with the principles of endogenous development.

The headquarters of the project is in Teheran which is mainly responsible for budgetary matters and liaison with other ministries. The total budget for March 1975 to March

FIG. 1 ALASHTAR (1:250000)

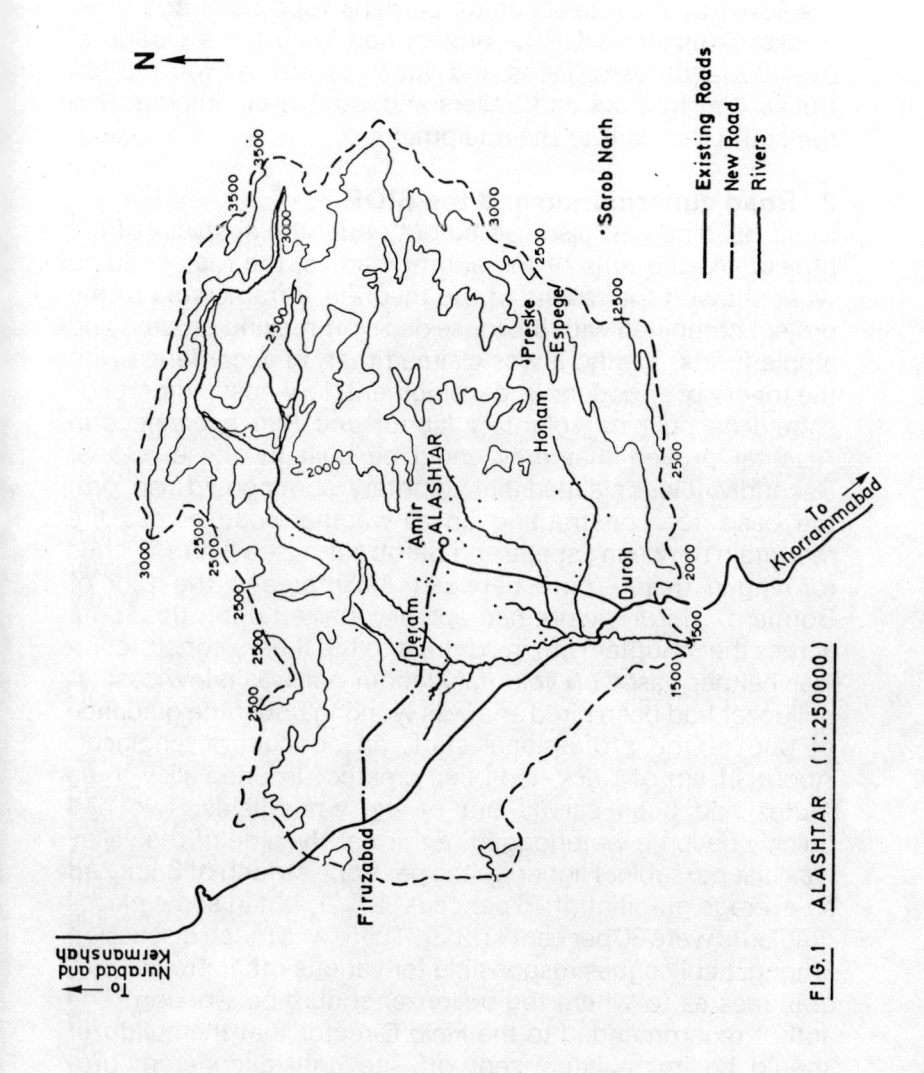

1976 was of the order of 10 million tomans ($1.4 million)[3]. Field programmes were devised and administered in Alashtar itself.

The large budget of the project allowed the purchase of significant amounts of equipment. Before the start of the project the town of Alashtar boasted perhaps four jeeps and three trucks. After one year the project had imported a garage of over 20 landrovers, jeeps and vans, as well as four 13-ton trucks, ten tractors and trailers and various equipment, and the staff attendant to the equipment.

## 2. Road construction and the SIDP

Road-building was also carried out under the auspices of the project. At the time of the author's arrival the road-building work showed the results of the theoretical framework of the project combined with the loose decision-making process and ample funds. Firstly, it was claimed that, in accordance with the theory of endogenous development, low-cost minor roads should be built by voluntary labour and that experience in Alashtar proved that they could be built by these means. Secondly, it was claimed that voluntary labour could also form the basis for constructing an all-weather road across the mountain between Espege and Sarob Narh (see figure 1), thus forming a major route between Alashtar and the City of Borujerd. Thirdly, work had actually started upon this route across the mountain but in contrast to the theory construction was neither based on voluntary labour nor was it low cost. A bulldozer had been hired and was working under the guidance of one of the professional staff, an agricultural engineer. About 21 km of track had been created. In one valley three routes had been carved out of the wheatfields: two had quickly become waterlogged, a third at the side of the valley was just passable. Higher up the pass one stretch of 3 km had an average gradient of 16 per cent (1:6.2), but in some places gradients were 30 per cent (1:3.3). There was much discussion amongst colleagues responsible for various other project programmes as to where the bulldozer should be working. The author recommended to the Field Director that the bulldozer should be immediately sent off site until a coherent programme be developed. This was for the following reasons:
    a) the visible product of the bulldozer's activity was neither low cost nor usable;

b) there was no plan of operation nor was equipment available to carry out the necessary back-up operations, particularly drainage and surfacing; equally, delays were anticipated in equipment supply and difficulties with regard to maintenance;
c) there was no map of the mountain route nor had any reconnaissance survey been carried out to establish preliminary routes or levels;
d) the spring rains were torrential; and the terrain soft sandstone: besides being idle during the rain, any work carried out by the bulldozer resulted, with each storm, in a morass. The work being carried out would have to be redone in the dry season. At the same time the higher reaches of track had become extremely dangerous to traverse;
e) as all the work being done by the D6 could be carried out manually, the money being spent on it could be used for hiring labour.

There were other reasons for a postponement of the road-building programme. While endogenous self-help is a noble idea and a case may be made for certain types of road building based on these principles, there were apparent constraints to the immediate implementation of such a programme. Firstly, in the face of visible evidence of the amount of money at the project's disposal (both in relation to the size of the staff and the vehicles imported), the local people were somewhat bemused at the need for ongoing voluntary labour on their part. Secondly, this attitude was exacerbated by evidence of the ready availability of equipment for construction. Equally, throughout the region it was frequently voiced that nowadays roads were built using machines (in particular bulldozers) and not men. Thirdly, neither the people nor project colleagues were unanimous as to the routes and types of road required. In sum, insufficient time and energy had been devoted to the careful pre-planning necessary to ensure the success of a self-help road-building project. However, there were two reasons why the bulldozer could not be returned. Firstly, a deposit of 50,000 tomans ($7,150) had been made for the D6. So far the bulldozer had not carried out 50,000 tomans of work. It was feared that should the bulldozer be returned the project would not be able to claim the balance from the equipment contractor.

Secondly, the bulldozer provided visible evidence that the project was active.

This, then, was the background to the initiation and implementation of labour-based road-building programme.

## 3. Social, environmental and technical factors

We now turn to a consideration of the various ways in which the standard of the road required by the project, a social decision, was affected by technical considerations and the environmental conditions of Alashtar. The method by which the road was to be built, voluntary participation, was affected firstly by the nature of the product required to fulfil the expected standard, and secondly by cultural factors. We will also show how interpretations of the theory of endogenous development made by professional colleagues and a certain bias in favour of machines militated against the adoption of a paid labour-based programme. At the same time the existing state of data on the relative merits of labour-and capital-intensive construction did not provide incontrovertible evidence of the technical efficiency of labour. Thus, in the face of opposition to any form of work using paid labour, it was not possible to present a clear-cut case for the adoption of a paid labour-based programme founded on its technical efficiency. Finally, we suggest the social factors which led to the eventual adoption of a paid labour-based programme.

### 3.1 *The standard of the road*

It has been mentioned above that the project was intent upon building low-cost minor roads.

Several environmental and technical factors suggested that the standard of road required for all-weather traffic was somewhat higher than that so far achieved through voluntary participation or the use of the D6. These factors included the following: the severe climatic conditions; the susceptibility of the terrain to these climatic conditions; the frequency of the cross-drainage necessitated by the existing irrigation system; the volume of tractor traffic and the destructive effect of tractors upon the existing tracks; the results of the traffic survey which showed that the new road would carry over 100 vehicles per day.

After consideration of the standard required — an all-weather road — it was concluded that the road should be built as close to secondary standards as the lack of planing allowed. On the basis of this assessment and the poor quality of the work that had been carried out previously, it was contended that just running a bulldozer through would neither provide an all-weather route for commercial traffic nor, in the long run, would it be low cost[4].

## 3.2 *The method of construction*
a) *Voluntary participation* — We have seen above that one of the major objectives of the project was to foster self-reliance through the means of voluntary participation. It was therefore expected that low-cost roads should also be built using voluntary participation. It was agreed that improved maintenance would result: villagers would be acquainted with the techniques of construction and proud of their work, therefore they would be able and willing to perform maintenance operations.

It became clear that the theory conflicted with reality. Firstly, whatever the level of socio-economic conditions prevailing in the region, the scale of voluntary participation expected of the people seemed to be high. Initially it had appeared reasonable that one might expect sporadic co-operation from the villagers in relation to certain village or personal amenities. But from the outset it seemed unreasonable to expect anything to be built by voluntary labour that was either time-consuming or that did not directly affect a particular village.

Secondly, the lack of response by the people to the calls for voluntary participation was not aided by the lack of enthusiasm amongst many of the project trainees themselves. This was in part the result of the fact that two of the three trainee groups were derived essentially from the better-educated and wealthy in the Alashtar region. Anthropological work[5] has shown that, amongst the better-educated and wealthy of Alashtar, manual labour is considered to be undignified: the project trainees were averse to implementing that part of the theory which emphasised the role of manual labour.

Further, remarks of the people concerning the project indicated that at a very basic level a lack of appreciation existed amongst them as to its purpose. The activities of the professional staff were interpreted as "All those engineers just eat and sleep and drive up and down in landrovers". And in relation to moral exhortations to participate voluntarily: "Those engineers get paid for not doing any work so why should I work and not get paid?" or "The project is part of the Government and the Government has lots of money so why should I work for nothing?". In addition, the project's concentration upon the need for voluntary work was interpreted as an attempt by the Government to foist third-class goods upon an unsuspecting public.

More fundamentally, the lack of voluntary participation reflected socio-economic characteristics. The low level of rural income in Lorestan is partly the result of seasonal unemployment. The climate of North and South-Western Iran (including Lorestan) is such that there is a slack period of six months in agriculture and at least four months in construction. The active periods for two of the major sources for earning income overlap. In Alashtar the intensive cycle of wheat, beans and sugarbeet means that during the best building weather agricultural activity is in progress. During the good weather, if other work is not available locally, those not employed in agriculture go to the cities, mostly to Teheran construction sites. However, the building season in Teheran is similar to that the Lorestan. During the long off-season unless workers migrate south there is very little work available and thus seasonal unemployment is high. While it is not possible to find data for Lorestan which clearly support such a commonly expressed criterion of visible underemployment/seasonal unemployment, a recent report concluded that, out of the 3.8 million agricultural workers in Iran, about 1 million "may thus be potentially unemployed, while those reported as seasonally unemployed are mainly landless labourers probably working much less than 100 days a year"[6].

Further to the short span of time available to accrue income, anthropological work in Lorestan[7], supported by other work in Iran[8], suggested that the vast majority of peasants were in debt to village headmen, local princes (Khans), or usurers. Thus, within the constraints of a low average income, the short span of time available for productive work, debt and social mores, there was little room for altruism during the best building weather.

There were therefore various socio-economic constraints upon the acceptance of the need for voluntary participation.

The theory of low-cost construction based upon voluntary participation conflicted with reality in the actual mode of operation. This was because expensive machinery had been hired without any coherent programme of operation. It was also proposed that further equipment be either bought or hired (graders, bulldozers, rollers, trucks). Voluntary labour was to complement equipment. However, the existing mode of operation and the equipment contemplated suggested that either construction would prove expensive or it would require inordinate amounts of voluntary labour.

The prevailing socio-economic conditions and the apparent need for employment creation were such that it was necessary to question whether most of the budget should be spent on buying or hiring of equipment or whether the funds might form the basis for an employment-creation programme. The title of the project suggested that it should include employment creation.

Socio-economic conditions indicated not only that extensive voluntary participation would not be possible but that there was a need for additional sources of income-generating employment in the region. The scale of funds at the project's disposal indicated that it possessed the resources to fulfil such a need. Consideration was therefore given to the role that might be played by a road-building programme based on paid labour.

b) *Technical efficiency of labour* — A feasibility study using the available literature was carried out. The results are summarised in tables 1-4. They show that for bulk excavation by labour, estimates vary from 0.12 $m^3$/hr to 2.28 $m^3$/hr (1,900 per cent variation) and for a D7 bulldozer from 64 $m^3$/hr to 410 $m^3$/hr (640 per cent variation).

Several utilisation rates were considered in calculating the cost of substitution of labour for equipment. For a utilisation rate of 2,500 hours per year, at a bulldozer cost of 32,600t/month ($4,650), the possible spectrum for substitution varies from 29.1 men costing 14,500t/month ($2,080) to 7,120 men costing 3,560,000t/month ($509,000).

Taking the figures at face value it was not possible to reach any conclusion in favour of labour at market prices. Equally, whereas the literature produced by the ILO is cautiously optimistic about the technical efficiency of labour substitution[9], the IBRD consider that modifications have to be made to existing techniques in order to make the substitution of labour for machines competitive[10]. However, certain factors suggested that the higher ranges of equipment productivity and utilisation rates would not apply in Alashtar. The project lacked maintenance facilities capable of ensuring high utilisation of equipment. Further, without continual supervision it was not possible to authenticate the amount of work carried out by the bulldozer. Moreover, in a situation where optimum planning did not prevail, it would be impossible to keep the dozer continually active. However, in the case of a hired machine such inactivity would have to be paid for by the project. Thus for various reasons it was considered that the utilisation rates would be lower than optimum.

Such reasoning led to the following interpretation of the data: for a utilisation rate of 1,500 hrs/yr, at a low- to middle-range labour productivity of 0.82 m$^3$/hr, and the lower order of bulldozer productivities, the following might apply: 48.8 men costing 24,400t/month ($3,490), 91.5 men at 45,700t/month ($6,530) or 109.5 men at 54,700t/month ($7,815) would be equivalent to a D7 bulldozer costing between 30,000 and 33,000t/month ($4,280 to $4,720).

The proposal that an experimental paid labour-based programme should be initiated was based upon the following factors:
  i) the role which could be played by a paid labour-based programme in regional employment creation;
  ii) the flexibility of labour as opposed to machinery in particular the bulldozer;
  iii) the heavy capital costs of equipment and the equally heavy, though somewhat milder, costs of maintenance;
  iv) Muller's contention that the use of labour-based methods had also resulted in improved maintenance because of a greater feeling of involvement[11];
  v) a case could be made for the technical efficiency of labour when compared with capital-intensive work.

c) *Voluntary labour v. paid labour v. equipment* — The proposal met with severe opposition. Firstly, it was widely held that the payment of labour conflicted with the basic premises of the project. Secondly, it was held that the productivity of men could not possibly compete with that of machines ... in particular the bulldozer[12]. The caveats presented as to long-term maintenance costs of equipment and average efficiency were received sceptically.

Repeated experiences in connection with the bulldozer led to the conclusion that both local people and the project staff were almost in awe of the machine. Time and time again the villagers approached the project for the use of the bulldozer for activities which were totally beyond its ability. It appeared that one reason for the maintest belief in the all-powerfulness of the bulldozer lay in its representation of modernity. To have work done by a bulldozer was the modern way of doing things.

Secondly, whereas the virtues of voluntary labour were declaimed, it was equally maintained that labour could not possibly compete with machines in respect of productivity. Paid labour was not only in contradiction to theory but more expensive and retrogressive as well. Voluntary labour in the context of a large equipment component was not.

The proposal that a labour-based programme be undertaken was therefore rejected out of hand on two basic grounds: paid labour was not in accordance with the theory of endogenous development and men could not compete with machines.

d) *Voluntary v. paid labour* — The project pressed ahead with road building by voluntary participation. Two factors resulted in the eventual adoption of an experimental programme using paid labour. The most important being the fact that, despite repeated attempts to recruit volunteers, no volunteers presented themselves. In addition, the employment that could be created for the money involved was pointed out, viz:

i) A full programme of capital-intensive work would utilise about 11,000t/day ($1,575). Implementing a programme where only 56 per cent of the cost was spent on labour would release 6,160t/day ($832) for their employment. At the current rate of 20t/day ($2.86) this would be sufficient to hire 308 people;

ii) the money presently spent upon the bulldozer alone could provide employment for 1,920/20 = 91 men per day.

The authorities were impressed by the sheer numbers of people who could be employed for the same amount of money as that being expended for the hiring of equipment. In the face of the continued lack of volunteers and the real need for visible product, they were sympathetic to the other arguments which had been put forward to support the initiation of an experimental programme of paid labour-based road construction. The combination of these factors caused the authorities to advocate the initiation of such a programme.

## 4. Summary of work programme and comment

### 4.1 *The work programme*

The programme consisted of the use of a combination of labour-based and equipment-intensive methods in the construction of some 15 kms of road over a 9-month period.

Detailed evaluations were made of the work completed (see table 5), the equipment and labour employed, the total costs and the various productivities for the following activities: embankment, gravelling, bridges and irrigation canal crossings. It must be pointed out that the size of staff did not permit accurate observation of quantities. The calculations were based on the daily reports compiled by the timekeeper and the head foreman, modified by observations made by the author.

### 4.2 *Comment on work completed*

First we will deal with aspects of the work which are to some extent quantifiable.

  a) It was calculated that the productivity of labour for work which was considered in the feasibility study to be "excavate and load", varied from 3.44 to 3.8 $m^3$/manday. The work was carried out under task work conditions which amounted to a working day of six hours. This is in the low range of labour productivities as derived from various sources and presented in table 4 (at this end of this chapter)[13].
  b) The productivity of the D155A-1 (320 hp) bulldozer was found to vary as follows:
  bulk excavation: (haul < 20 m) : 105 $m^3$/hr; (average haul 50 m) : 42 $m^3$/hr;
  excavate and shape embankment: (haul < 20 m) : 41.7-67 $m^3$/hr.

These results vary from *3.6* to *9.1* per cent of the maximum manufacturer's productivities quoted in IBRD Technical Memorandum No. 7[14]. The productivity of the D6 (140 hp) for excavating and shaping the embankment (haul < 20 m) was 27.5 m³/hr or *5.5* per cent of the maximum quoted in Technical Memorandum No. 7[15]. Two points may be ventured in respect of the extremely low productivities obtained by the bulldozers. Firstly, the area adjacent to the route which was encroached upon during construction was five to ten times greater in the case of the bulldozer than in the case of labour. Secondly, the system of work employed by the dozer in making the embankment entailed a greater bulk movement of earth than that used by labour-based methods. The road was created by a series of movements entailing first the dumping of earth in large mounds followed by the shaping of these mounds into place.

c) It was possible to compare unit costs of labour and bulldozer for embankment construction. For labour this varied from 7 to 7.35t/m³ (1 to 1.05$m³), whilst that for the bulldozer amounted to 3.83t/m[16]. At the rates charged for the bulldozer it can be seen that the labour-based work was distinctly inefficient: 83 to 92 per cent more expensive[17].

It must be stressed that the rate charged through the Governor General's office for a 320 HP bulldozer (D155A-1) was 140t/hr ($20). The author has not been able to ascertain the market price of the same piece of equipment but the following comparisons may be made: from a rental contractor a "special price for the project" of a 270 hp (D8) had been 192t/hr ($27.5/hr), the normal rate from the same contractor being 220t/hr ($31.5/hr). By comparison with this rate it may be seen that the rate through the Governor General's office was generous, to say the least.

On the basis of rental contractors' rates for a D7 and a D8, the rate for a D155A-1 (320 hp) would be of the order of 265t/hr (37.90/hr). Using such a rate we find that the cost productivity of the bulldozer amounts to 6.83t/m³ ($0.98/m³), i.e. *2.5* to *7.5* per cent cheaper than labour. Excluding the roller common to both we find the cost productivity of the bulldozer amounts to 6.34t/m³, i.e. equipment becomes 3.1 to 3.6 per cent more expensive than labour. These estimates do not include transport costs (equivalent to two days' work). Thus, at prevailing market prices for the same piece of equipment, labour-intensive work becomes far more competitive than at the rates through the Governor General's office.

d) In the spreading operation, productivity amounted to 2.95 m³/man-day. However, it is felt that this productivity was severely inhibited by the frequent passage of trucks which disrupted the work.

e) The costs of gravel haulage amounted to 23 per cent of the cost (excluding river re-route and bridges).
Due to the loaders being supplied as part of the package from the Governor General's office, it was not possible to substitute labour for the loading process. Loading and haulage amounted to 28.4 per cent of the cost: at market prices this would amount to 32.5 per cent.

f) The method of constructing irrigation canal crossings based upon second-hand barrels was found to be satisfactory. The cost of one of these amounted to $147 as opposed to $345 using 45 cm diameter reinforced concrete pipes.

g) Self-driven vibrating rollers were bought in place of the tractor-drawn rollers specified. Not only were these vibrating rollers extremely sensitive — the smaller one was almost permanently out of action — but they could only travel on a level roadway which considerably restricted manoeuvreability.

h) Excluding the cost of re-routing the river and building the bridges, but including an estimate for completion of gravelling, the over-all cost per kilometre amounted to 105,500 tomans ($15,000). Using market rates for the hire of the bulldozer, trucks and loaders, the over-all cost per kilometre would have been 122,750 tomans ($17,525). These figures are well below contractors' estimates for similar standard roads in neighbouring areas, these being of the order of 200,000 to 230,000 tomans per kilometre ($28,600 to $32,800).

i) Tables 6 and 7 summarise the employment creation in man-days per kilometre for the different tasks and for different combinations of the tasks. For the section of the road in which the embankment, spreading and water crossings were constructed by essentially labour-based means, the employment creation amounted to approximately 2,800 man-days per kilometre. For the section in which only spreading and water crossings were carried out by labour-based methods and the rest constructed by capital-intensive methods, the employment creation amounted to approximately 840 man-days per kilometre. It was possible to compare the costs per kilometre of construction of the whole road by the different methods, and the relative proportions of labour and equipment. Excluding overhead costs (salaried officials) a breakdown is given in table 5 and the results are summarised in table 8. The actual cost of the section in which embankment construction, water crossings and spreading were carried out by essentially labour-based means was 101,880 tomans per kilometre ($14,550). The actual cost of the section in which only spreading and water crossings were carried out by labour-based means and the rest was constructed by capital-intensive methods was 81,930 tomans per kilometre ($11,700).

We see that the actual cost of construction using a higher proportion of capital to labour was 19.5 per cent cheaper than that using nearly equal proportions of labour and capital. However, at market rates for equipment we find that the cost of the section which was constructed using a higher ratio of labour to capital would have amounted to 112,575 tomans per kilometre ($16,090), while the section constructed with a higher proportion of capital would have cost 113,175 tomans ($16,170). In this case, the section completed using a higher proportion of labour would have been 0.5 per cent cheaper.

Experience in the Alashtar programme also contributes to the less quantifiable aspects of the on-going debate as to the relative merits and demerits of labour-based and capital-intensive methods.

   a) During the height of the agricultural season there was no difficulty in recruiting 100 men for the small labour-intensive programme. Later, when the workforce was expanded, agricultural activity was still in progress. No difficulty was experienced in hiring 288 men.

By contrast, during the best building weather, there were often delays in the delivery of machinery. Therefore, in Alashtar, greater difficulty was experienced in locating machinery than men.

b) Some idea of the utilisation rates of equipment and the maintenance required has been given above. Mention should also be made of the repercussive effect that breakdowns had upon the work.

c) In Alashtar, when the programme or the weather changed, men could be laid off and recruited when necessary. By comparison, if one wished to lay off equipment for a short period, then one had to pay for the period laid off. If one wished to lay off equipment for a long period, then one could not be sure of being able to obtain it again on demand.

d) It has been suggested[18] that the ease of labour mobilisation and the lower overheads might be offset by the costs and organisational problems of running a large labour camp. In Alashtar this was not the case as the men were recruited from villages alongside the route. By contrast, it was found necessary to run a small road camp for the equipment operators and many difficulties were experienced in keeping them satisfied with the standard of food and accommodation.

It would seem therefore that for a small isolated programme without a rigorous work schedule (and limited workshop facilities), the hiring of machines is potentially more expensive than the hiring of men.

4.3 *Labour organisation*

The substitution of men for machines in Alashtar was facilitated by the fact that until abour 12 years ago, roads in Lorestan were built using labour as a major component. Many of the men were therefore familiar with the work.

Perhaps more important is that, in Alashtar, one of the forms of labour organisation is based upon gangleaders. Gangleaders find the work, supply the labour, and themselves supervise the working of the gang. As such, the reintroduction of labour-based work is not dependent upon extensive training in labour organisation or the chance discovery of experienced foremen.

With a small staff it was necessary to promote workers who were willing and capable. It was found that unless care was taken to ensure that the delegation of authority was understood by all concerned (over 300 people), those to whom authority was delegated were unable to act. Conversely, once authority had been acknowledged, many of the new men were able to function very well.

Finally, while costs of labour mobilisation and overheads were very low, recruiting labour from villages along the route did result in a certain amount of friction as to who was entitled to work on a particular stretch of road.

## 5. **Conclusions**

5.1 *Conclusions related to technical aspects*
   a) At the hiring rates available through the Governor General's office (almost half the market price), it was not possible to achieve a technically efficient substitution of manual labour for machines. At market prices, however, estimates showed equipment-intensive methods to vary between 3.6 per cent more expensive and 7.5 per cent cheaper than labour-based methods.
   b) Productivities for earthmoving equipment were found to be as low as 5 to 10 per cent of that of the maximum manufacturer's data quoted in the World Bank Technical Memoranda No. 7[19].
   c) The variety of labour productivities presented in the literature was so varied that probably a month of work on site is necessary before an adequate estimate may be obtained for planning purposes.
   d) In a small isolated community development project machine-intensive work is potentially more expensive than labour.

5.2 *Conclusions related to social aspects of the work*
   a) Under the particular conditions obtaining in Alashtar, it was found difficult to introduce labour-based methods for the following reasons:

i) the professional staff were committed to the concept of voluntary work;
ii) the professional staff found it extremely difficult to accept that labour could be as technically efficient as machines;
iii) foremen tended to view labour-based work as giving them less status than equipment-intensive work;
iv) villagers and townspeople echoed professional staff opinion as to the manifold advantages of the bulldozer over labour. The villagers could see that the project had financial resources for equipment and consequently saw no necessity for *voluntary* labour-based methods of construction. The bias was removed once labour changed from voluntary to paid.

Under these conditions, it is considered that it is no more difficult to organise a labour-based work programme than any other civil engineering programme. If anything, the equipment side of the project provided more problems for the engineer.

b) Labour-based construction has often been seen to be particularly relevant to capital-scarce and labour-abundant economies. It might be argued that the material context of a capital-rich and rapidly modernising economy like Iran obviates the need for labour-based work. However, in Alashtar, the response to labour recruitment was such as to indicate that at the regional level an abundance of labour still exists. Within such a context the expansion of labour-based construction would be valid.

c) Seasonal variation of labour has often been seen as a restriction upon labour-based construction. Experience in Alashtar suggests that a quite substantial body of men could be hired for the whole building season. They could be employed in smaller teams to carry out particular parts of work scattered along the route — such as bridge construction, irrigation canal crossings and the more complicated pieces of embankment work.

d) Experience in Alashtar certainly substantiates the statements in the IBRD Phase I report that labour-based work should be "socially acceptable to the people of the country"[20].

Equally, that for labour-based work to be successful it should be "actively supported ... at the highest possible level"[21].

**Notes and references**

[1] The author wishes to acknowledge the significant roles played by the Field Director, Dr. M.T. Farvar (now Vice-Chancellor, Bu-Ali Sina University, Hamadan) and the Head Foreman, Mr. Shaverdi. Without their co-operation it would not have been possible to carry out the work described in this paper. He also wishes to thank Dr. G. Edmonds and Mr. P.A. Green for their assistance. Finally, he would like to thank Carol Gregor McCutcheon for her sustained interest through several drafts.

[2] For an overview of SIDP the reader is referred to M.T. Farvar and C. Razawi-Farvar,."The lessons of Lorestan, achievements and shortcomings of a project in endogenous development" *CERES* 9 (2), March-April 1976, pp. 44-47. In the present introduction the author has presented only the barest outline of the SIDP concentrating upon aspects pertinent to the road-building programme.

[3] The rial is the unit of currency in Iran. In 1977, 70 rials = $1. Colloquially the toman is used; 1 toman = 10 rials. The author has referred to tomans throughout the paper; 7 tomans = $1.

[4] The first 9 km of track originally created by the D6 had to be graded or dozed four times in as many months.

[5] Jacob Black, "Tyranny as a strategy for survival in an 'egalitarian' society: Luri facts versus an anthropological mystique", *MAN*, 7 (4), Dec. 1972, 614-634. Jacob Black-Michaud, "An ethnographic and ecological survey of Luristan, Western Persia: modernisation in a nomadic pastoral society", *Middle Eastern Studies*, 10 (2), May 1974, 210-228.

[6] Employment and Incomes Policies for Iran, Geneva, ILO, 1973, p. 27.

[7] Jacob Black, op. cit.

[8] N.R. Keddie, "The Iranian village before and after land reform", in Henry Berstein: *Underdevelopment and Development, The Third World Today, Selected Reading* (Harmondsworth, Penguin, 1973), pp. 152-174.

[9] Deepak Lal, *Men or Machines* (Geneva, ILO, 1978).

[10] *Study of the Substitution of Labour for Equipment in Civil Construction, Phase II — Final Report* (IBRD, Staff Working Paper No. 172, Jan. 1974).

[11] Muller, "Labour-intensive methods in low-cost road construc-

tion: a case study", *International Labour Review*, 101, Apr. 1970, pp. 359-375.

[12] It was also held that it must be easier to organise a small team of equipment operators than a large labour force, which indicated the scale of voluntary activity anticipated and therefore the equipment-intensive nature of the programme envisaged.

[13] See also "Report of first road demonstration project", Technical Memorandum No. 9 (IBRD, Aug. 1975), p. 19.

[14] "Productivity rates of earthmoving machines", Technical Memorandum No. 7 (IBRD, May 1975), p. 43.

[15] ibid., p. 42.

[16] Excluding the roller common to both methods, we find that labour varies from 6.12 to 6.15t/$m^3$ (0.875 to 0.878$/$m^3$), while the bulldozer productivity amounts to 3.35t/$m^3$, i.e. 83 to 83.4 per cent more expensive. It is perhaps worth noting the obvious that the percentage of equipment cost increased with the decrease in the number of people employed to the detriment of labour cost productivities: for 120 men equipment was only 25.9 per cent of total costs, for 70 men it rose to 35.5 per cent.

[17] Irvin, op. cit., p. 34. Here 67.5 rials = $1, i.e. 6.75t = $1.

[18] IBRD (1971), op. cit., p. 91.

[19] IBRD (May 1975), op. cit.

[20] IBRD (Oct. 1971), op. cit.

[21] IBRD. ibid.

Table 1: Productivity estimates from various sources for a 180 HP bulldozer

| Source | $m^3$/hr. for haul up to 20 m |
|---|---|
| Muller (70)[1] | 27.5 |
| Lal (74)[2] | 64.0 |
| Lal (74)[3] | 91.0 |
| Geddes (67)[4] | 95.0 |
| Lal (74)[5] | 120.0 |
| 35% manufacturer's maximum for D7[6] | 143.5 |
| 45% manufacturer's maximum for D7[7] | 184.0 |
| Lal (74)[8] | 190.0 |
| Peurifoy (70)[9] | 225.0 |
| Manufacturer's maxima as quoted by Lal (74)[10] | |
|     Komatsu D80A-12 | 235.0 |
|     Caterpillar D7 | 410.0 |
| 25% manufacturer's maximum for D7[11] | 205.0 |
| Manufacturer's maxima as quoted by IBRD Tech. Memo No. 7[12] | |
|     Komatsu D804.12 | 603.0 |
|     Caterpillar | 820.0 |

[1] Muller (1970), productivity derived from data on p. 236; unfortunately Muller does not clarify whether he used a D4 or a D7.

[2] Lal (1974), lower range estimate for D7 on p. 57.

[3] Lal (1974), average estimate for D7 on p. 57.

[4] Geddes (1967), productivities given on p. 161 for a 35 hp D4, a 55 hp D6, an 80 hp D7, and a 113 hp D8; productivity in table derived by extrapolation to 180 hp.

[5] Lal (1974), upper range estimate for D7 on p. 57. Irvin (75), p. 141, gives an estimate for a D8 which adjusted using Lal's graph on p. 57 gives the same productivities.

[6] Lal (1974), pp. 153 and 155, Lal recommends that productivities are of the order of 35 per cent of Caterpillar maxima.

[7] Lal (1974), p. 22, "a figure of 40-50 per cent of the published productivity rates would provide a realistic degradation factor for operating equipment in a less developed country". The IBRD report only refers to Caterpillar equipment bulldozers. The productivity given is derived from 45 per cent of the data in Lal (74), p. 155.

[8] Lal (1974), p. 41, gives "ex ante estimate" for D7 and 100 m haul; above figures derived by adjusting the 20 m using Lal (74), p. 57.

[9] Peurifoy (1970), p. 164. The data in Peurifoy are for tracked bulldozers varying from 32 hp to 132 hp; productivity in table derived by extrapolation to 180 hp.

[10] Lal (1974), p. 155.

[11] IBRD (1975), Tech. Memo No. 7, p. 21. IBRD recommend that outputs are 25 per cent of Caterpillar maxima. It should be noted that the maximum in TM No. 7 are double those quoted by Lal (74), p. 155.

[12] ibid., pp. 42 and 43.

*Table 2: Estimates of monthly productivities for various utilisation rates*

| Source | Hrs./yr.<br>Hrs./mth.<br>m$^3$/hr. | 1 000[13]<br>83.4 | 1 500[14]<br>125 | 2 000[15]<br>166.5 | 2 500<br>208 |
|---|---|---|---|---|---|
| Muller[1] | 27.5 | 2 270 | 3 430 | 4 580 | 5 720 |
| Lal (74)[2] | 64.0 | 5 340 | 8 000 | 10 670 | 13 350 |
| Lal (74)[3] | 91.0 | | | | |
| Geddes (67)[4] | 95.0 | 7 940 | 11 900 | 15 850 | 19 750 |
| Lal (74)[5] | 120.0 | 10 000 | 15 000 | 20 000 | 25 000 |
| 35% (Lal)[6] | 143.5 | 11 950 | 17 950 | 23 900 | 29 800 |
| 45% (Lal)[7] | 184.0 | 15 300 | 22 900 | 30 600 | 38 200 |
| Lal (74)[8] | 190.0 | | | | |
| Peurifoy[9] | 225.0 | 18 750 | 28 100 | 37 500 | 46 800 |
| Manuf. ex Lal[10] | | | | | |
| Komatsu | 235.0 | 19 600 | 29 300 | 39 100 | 48 800 |
| D7 | 410.0 | 34 200 | 51 200 | 68 300 | 85 200 |
| 25% manuf.[11] (IBRD) | 205.0 | 17 100 | 25 600 | 34 100 | 42 700 |
| Komatsu (IBRD)[12] | 603.0 | 50 400 | 75 500 | 100 500 | 125 800 |
| D7 (IBRD) | 820.0 | 68 300 | 102 500 | 136 500 | 171 000 |
| Rates t/hr. (Irvin) | | 340 | 240 | 190.5 | 160.6 |

[1-12] As for table 1.
[13] Lower range utilisation reported by IBRD (74).
[14] Border roads IBRD (75).
[15] Upper range also IBRD (75), also Peurifoy (70).
[16] Irvin (75).

*Table 3: Bulk excavation*

| Sources | m$^3$/hr. | m$^3$/day | m$^3$/mth. | Soil type | Method of payment |
|---|---|---|---|---|---|
| IBRD (74)[1] | 0.12 | 0.96 | 24 | Ord. | |
| Lal (73)[2] | 0.216 | 1.73 | 43.2 | | |
| Muller (70)[3] | 0.337 | 2.7 | 67.5 | | |
| Lal (74)[4] | 0.443 | | | 6 | Daily |
| Lal (74) | 0.535 | | | 5 | Daily |
| Muller (70)[5] | 0.55 | 4.4 | 110 | | |
| Lal (74)[4] | 0.785 | | | 6 | Task |
| Lal (74) | 0.82 | | | ( 4<br>( 6 | Daily,<br>piece |
| Lal (74) | 0.945 | | | 5 | Task |
| Lal (74) | 0.99 | | | 5 | Piece |
| Lal (74) | 1.235 | | | 3 | Daily |
| Lal (74) | 1.44 | 11.5 | 228 | 4 | Task |
| Lal (74) | 1.51 | | | 4 | Piece |
| IBRD (74)[6] | 1.66 | 13.25 | 331.5 | Ord. | |
| Lal (74)[4] | 2.2 | | | 3 | Task |
| Lal (74) | 2.28 | 18.25 | 455 | 3 | Piece |
| Allal and Edmonds[7] | 1.25<br>0.57 | | 118 | 2 | Daily |

[1] IBRD (74), p. 22, lower range.
[2] Lal (73), provisional draft of *Men or machines*, p. 44, estimate for excavation of structure.
[3] Muller (70), p. 366.
[4] Lal (74), pp. 138 and 139.
[5] Muller (70), p. 366, derived from data on p. 366.
[6] IBRD (74), p. 22, upper range.
[7] Allal and Edmonds (75), p. 123, table 5.2, European Standard.

*Table 4:* Labour productivity estimates from various sources

2. Excavate and load

|  | $m^3$/hr. | $m^3$/day | $m^3$/mth. | Soil type | Method |
|---|---|---|---|---|---|
| Lal (74)[1] | .3 | | | 5 | Daily |
| Lal (73)[2] | .375 | 3.0 | | | |
| Lal (74)[1] | .39 | | | 4 | Daily |
| Geddes (67)[3] | .42 | 3.36 | 84 | Gravel and compact soil | |
| Lal (74)[1] | .433 | | | 3 | Daily |
| Lal (74) | .475 | | | 5 | Task |
| Geddes (67)[4] | .477 | 3.81 | 95 | Gravel and compact soil | |
| Lal (74)[1] | .55 | | | 5 | Piece |
| Lal (74) | .57 | | | 4 | Task |
| Lal (74)[5] | .625 | 5.0 | 125 | | |
| Geddes (67)[6] | .63 | 5.04 | 126 | Sandy clay | |
| Lal (74)[1] | .664 | | | 3 | Task |
| (74) | .68 | | | 4 | Piece |
| Geddes (67)[7] | .764 | 6.11 | 153 | | |
| Lal (74)[1] | .8 | | | 3 | Piece |
| Lal (73)[8] | .85 | 6.8 | | Common soil | |
| Lal (73)[8] | 1.0 | 8.0 | | soft sort | |
| Allal and Edmonds[9] | 1.1 | | | 3 | Piece |

[1] Lal (74), derived from data on pp. 138–141. Productivity ratios for excavation piece : task : daily : : 1.85 : 1.77 : 1.00. Productivity ratios for loading to 1 m piece : task : daily : : 1.85 : 1.42 : 1.00.
[2] Lal (73), provisional draft of Lal (74), p. 60.
[3] Geddes (67), p. 148 to vehicles.
[4] ibid. to barrows.
[5] Lal (74), p. 41 ex ante estimate.
[6] Geddes (67), p. 148 to vehicles.
[7] ibid to barrows.
[8] Lal (73), p. 60.
[9] Allal and Edmonds (75), table 5.4, p. 124.

*Table 5:* Costs per kilometre of various methods of construction

1. Labour-intensive embankment and spreading, and capital-intensive excavation, load and haul
   Actual costs per km

|  | Labour | Equipment | Materials | Total |
|---|---|---|---|---|
| Embankment | 34 200 | 11 850 |  |  |
| Excavation |  | 2 680 |  |  |
| Load and haul |  | 29 400 |  |  |
| Spreading | 10 160 | 1 130 |  |  |
| Canal crossings | 3 580 | 3 760 | 5 120 |  |
| Totals | 47 940 | 48 820 | 5 120 | 101 880 |
| % | 47.0 | 48.0 | 5.0 | 100 |

2. Capital-intensive embankment, excavation, load and haul, and labour-intensive spreading
   Actual costs per km

| Embankment |  | 26 100 |  |  |
|---|---|---|---|---|
| Excavation |  | 2 680 |  |  |
| Load and haul |  | 29 400 |  |  |
| Spreading | 10 160 | 1 130 |  |  |
| Canal crossings | 3 580 | 3 760 | 5 120 |  |
| Totals | 13 740 | 63 070 | 5 120 | 81 930 |
| % | 16.8 | 77.0 | 6.2 | 100 |

3. Labour-intensive embankment and spreading, and capital-intensive excavation, load and haul
   Costs per km *at market rates*

| Embankment | 34 200 | 11 850 |  |  |
|---|---|---|---|---|
| Excavation |  | 5 075 |  |  |
| Load and haul |  | 37 700 |  |  |
| Spreading | 10 160 | 1 130 |  |  |
| Canal crossings | 3 580 | 3 760 | 5 120 |  |
| Totals | 47 940 | 59 515 | 5 120 | 112 575 |
| % | 42.5 | 52.9 | 4.6 | 100 |

4. Capital-intensive embankment, excavation, load and haul, and labour-intensive spreading
   Costs per km *at market rates*

|  | Labour | Equipment | Materials | Total |
|---|---|---|---|---|
| Embankment |  | 46 650 |  |  |
| Excavation |  | 5 075 |  |  |
| Load and haul |  | 37 700 |  |  |
| Spreading | 10 160 | 1 130 |  |  |
| Canal crossings | 3 580 | 3 760 | 5 120 |  |
| Totals | 13 740 | 94 315 | 5 120 | 113 175 |
| % | 12.1 | 83.4 | 4.5 | 100 |

*Table 6: Employment creation per task*

| Task | | | | | Labour | | | | |
|---|---|---|---|---|---|---|---|---|---|
| | Length m | | Vol m3 | No | Skilled Mandays | Cost | No | Unskilled Mandays | Cost |
| *Embankment* | | | | | | | | | |
| 1. Total | 3500 | | 2300 | 1 | 60 | 2100 | 112 | 6700 | 117500 |
| Labour | (2620) | | (17450) | (1) | (60) | (2310) | (70.5) | (4640) | (81200) |
| Intensive | 6120 | | 40650 | | 120 | | | 11340 | |
| 2. Total | 1520 | | 4070 | | | | | | |
| Capital | 1200 | | 11350 | | | | | | |
| Intensive | 2720 | | 15420 | | | | | | |
| 3. Mixed | 3240 | | 21200 | 1 | 27 | 945 | 136.5 | 3680 | 64300 |
| *Gravelling* | | | | | | | | | |
| 1. Excavation | | | 18240 | | | | | | |
| 2. Haulage | | | | | | | | | |
| (a) (i) Base | 5500 | a) 12.5 | 13500 | | | | | | |
| | 4000 | a) 25 | | | | | | | |
| (ii) Fill | | | 2240 | | | | | | |
| (b) Base | 1250 | a) 25 | 2500 | | | | | | |
| *Spreading* | | | | | | | | | |
| (i) | 5500m | a) 12.5 | 16000 | 1 | 60 | 2100 | 89 | 5347 | 94500 |
| (ii) | 5250m | a) 25 | | | | | | | |
| *Water Crossings* | No | | Length | | | | | | |
| 1. Canal Crossings | 78 | | 10.5 m | 1 | 156 | 5450 | 9 | 1404 | 25350 |
| 2. Canal Crossings | 8 | | 9 | 1 | 16 | 560 | 9 | 144 | 2600 |
| 3. Bridges (a) | 1 | | 13 | 1 | 60 | 2100 | | 484 | 8467 |
| (b) | 1 | | 11.5 | 1 | 59 | 2065 | | 468 | 8186 |

*including gift to driver

| | Equipment | | | Materials | Employment Creation (Skilled and Unskilled) | | |
|---|---|---|---|---|---|---|---|
| Type | No | Skilled Mandays | Cost | (Cost at Approx. Market Rates) | Total Mandays | Mandays Per KM | Mandays Per M3 |
| Tractors | 4 | 240 | 41450 | | 7000 | 2000 | 0.279 |
| Rollers | (4) | (264) | (45960) | | (4970) | (1898) | (0.283) |
| D6 | 1 | 15 | 28800 | (18000) | 11970 | 1955 | 0.294 |
| D155A-1 | 2 | 34 | 39756* | (72000) | | | |
| R90 | 1 | 17 | 5440 | | 51 | 42.5 | |
| D155A-1 | 2 | 31 | 27160* | (49300) | | | 0.0045 |
| R90 | 1 | 27 | 8640* | | | | |
| Tractors | 3 | 81 | 9990 | | 3846 | 1190 | 0.1815 |
| D155A-1 | 2 | 29 | 25444* | (46110) | 29 | 3.05 | |
| Trucks | 5 | 275 | 176000 | | | | |
| Loaders | 2 | 110 | 41250 | | 385 | 40.5 | 0.0245 |
| | | | | (358050) | | | |
| Trucks | 2 | 42 | 42000 | | | | |
| Loaders | 1 | 21 | 10500 | | | | |
| Gift | | | 10000 | | | | |

|  | Equipment | | | Materials | Employment Creation (Skilled and Unskilled) | | |
|---|---|---|---|---|---|---|---|
| Type | No | Skilled Mandays | Cost | (Cost at Approx. Market Rates) | Total Mandays | Mandays Per KM | Mandays Per M3 |
| Bowsers | 1 | 19 | 3040 | | 5450 | 573 | 0.341 |
| R90 | 1 | 24 | 7680 | | | | |
| | | | 24960 | 24725 | 1720 | 181 | |
| | | | 10815 | 23920 | | | |
| | | | 11550 | 46502 | | | |
| | | | 10360 | 38645 | | | |

*Table 7: Comparison of employment creation per kilometre*

1. *Labour-intensive embankment and spreading and capital-intensive excavation, load and haul*

|  | Mandays per km |
|---|---|
| Embankment | 2 000 |
| Excavation | 3.1 |
| Load and haul | 40.5 |
| Spreading | 573 |
| Canal crossings | 181 |
|  | 2 797.6 |

2. *Capital-intensive embankment, excavation, load and haul, and labour-intensive spreading*

|  | Mandays per km |
|---|---|
| Embankment | 42.5 |
| Excavation | 3.1 |
| Load and haul | 40.5 |
| Spreading | 573 |
| Canal crossings | 181 |
|  | 840.1 |

*Table 8: Comparison of various methods of construction costs and proportion per km*

1. *Labour-intensive embankment and spreading, and capital-intensive excavation, load and haul*
Actual costs per km

|  | Labour | Equipment | Materials | Total |
|---|---|---|---|---|
| Cost | 47 940 | 48 820 | 5 120 | 101 880 |
| % | 47.0 | 48.0 | 5.0 | 100 |

2. Capital-intensive embankment, excavation, load and haul, and labour-intensive spreading
Actual costs per km

|      | Labour | Equipment | Materials | Total |
|------|--------|-----------|-----------|-------|
| Cost | 13 740 | 63 070    | 5 120     | 81 930 |
| %    | 16.8   | 77.0      | 6.2       | 100   |

3. *Labour-intensive embankment and spreading, and capital-intensive excavation load and haul*
Cost per km at market rates

|      | Labour | Equipment | Materials | Total |
|------|--------|-----------|-----------|-------|
| Cost | 47 940 | 59 515    | 5 120     | 112 575 |
| %    | 42.5   | 52.9      | 4.6       | 100   |

4. *Capital-intensive embankment, excavation, load and haul, and labour-intensive spreading*

|      | Labour | Equipment | Materials | Total |
|------|--------|-----------|-----------|-------|
| Cost | 13 740 | 94 315    | 5 120     | 113 175 |
| %    | 12.1   | 83.4      | 4.5       | 100   |

## EDITORS' SUMMARY

Whilst the studies and programmes executed, by the ILO and the World Bank in particular, have shown that labour-based methods are technically and economically viable, there is a natural reluctance, particularly on the part of engineers, to adopt their use. Robert McCutcheon's description of the project in Iran illustrates this point very well. The project staff clearly felt that labour-intensive methods were useful for self-help programmes which would encourage popular participation but not as effective alternatives to equipment. It is also fair to point out, in mitigation of this attitude, that previous experience with the use of labour-intensive methods particularly on major relief programmes, tended to support their basic assumption that these methods were neither technically nor economically effective. Whilst programmes such as that described by Glaister in Afghanistan are extremely useful in mobilising human resources and endeavour in the rural areas, their very nature is such that they are unlikely to be economically justifiable.

The reluctance of engineers to accept that labour-based methods are a viable technological alternative is most effectively overcome by demonstration. Recent work on appropriate construction technology has had many aspects, however, perhaps the most important single element has been the physical proof that labour-based methods can be used for a wide range of construction activities without any reduction in standard or increase in cost (whether measured in economic or financial terms). Furthermore, this conclusion has been reached not only from studies carried out in experimental conditions but also in fully operational construction projects. Nevertheless, the suggestion that we should think of these methods as feasible alternatives to the use of equipment rather than useful methods of providing employment and income does present other major problems. In the first place, it means that their application has to be integrated into the institutional framework of the construction sector. It requires that the procedures and systems, developed principally for the use of equipment-intensive methods, have to be modified to incorporate the use of labour-based methods. This is well illustrated in Bertil Nilsson's paper, in particular in relation to training, procurement and administration.

Above all what emerges, in particular from the descriptions of the operational labour-based programmes, is *the need for commitment*. This is true whatever level is concerned. It is particularly vital that the government should be seen to be supporting the implementation of labour-based programmes: this not only confers respectability but should ensure that problems which will inevitably arise in their implementation receive sympathetic consideration. This could be reflected in the acceptance of tendering by specifications for hand tools, as in Kenya, or more broadly, in the endorsement of a programme by a senior politician, as in Iran.

At the other end of the scale there needs to be commitment at the grass-roots level. Unless the people themselves are convinced that the benefits of road construction will come to them, there is little likelihood of them being motivated to work effectively. The level of this popular participation can, of course, vary and leads logically to a socio-political discussion which is outside the scope of this book. However, there are clearly advantages and disadvantages whatever level is chosen. In Afghanistan, George Glaister found that where resources are extremely scarce there is great advantage in mobilising those of the rural population by giving them the responsibility for the selection and planning of work. However, there are serious disadvantages too, in that the people will only construct that which they feel is necessary and not that which might be necessary for safety and the type of traffic. In Mexico, on the other hand, whilst the people proposed and selected the roads, a contract was then made between the local community and the Direccion General de Caminos Rurales (DGCR) which ensured that the requisite number of labourers was available to construct a road whose standards were laid down by the DGCR. The basic difference, of course, between the Mexican and Afghanistan programmes is that in the former the labourers are paid whilst in the latter they are not. This point is strongly made by McCutcheon. When the programme was based on self-help the villagers were unwilling to work for they could see that money was available to pay for machinery. When this money was utilised to pay labourers there was no difficulty in obtaining an adequate work force.

The move from equipment-intensive to labour-based methods therefore has ramifications outside the merely technical. Popular participation and commitment become important even in the decision-making process.

In his discussion of the private sector, Angus Austen also raises the question of commitment. If there is a real desire on the part of the government to develop the domestic construction sector then this implies a recognition of the biases in the procedures and systems against such development. He suggests that appropriate construction technology would be one means of allowing the small contractor to grow. The World Bank have also suggested that for certain countries to eliminate bias against the use of labour-based methods a "neutralisation" procedure could be adopted in the contractual process. This, of course, is a useful starting point but if labour-based methods are to achieve their full potential then the procedures and systems will have to be modified throughout so that a rational choice can be made by all involved in the construction process.

Even if the commitment exists, there still remains the detailed problems of modifying or reassessing all aspects of the construction process in relation to the application of labour-based methods. The main aspects of this are covered in Chapter 2. Nevertheless, they are reinforced by the evidence from the various programmes described. In relation to planning and administration it is interesting to compare the programmes in India, Kenya, Afghanistan and Mexico. The Border Roads Organisation is run on military lines and as such the hierarchy of responsibility is very clearly defined. It is also heavily centralised as the level of supervisory and administrative personnel indicates. At the other extreme, in the Afghanistan programme, the responsibility is devolved to the workers and the Rural Development Department officials act only as advisers not supervisors. The question of how far responsibility should be devolved depends on many factors not least the nature of the programme. The Kenya Rural Access Roads Programme (RARP) covers the whole country and with such a dispersal of sites it is natural that the engineers in the field should have a large measure of responsibility. The same applies to the Mexican programme, however there is one basic difference. The RARP field structure is totally separated from that of the provincial engineer, who is the regional representative and executing agency of the Ministry of Works. Conversely, the Mexican programme is run through the field offices of the DGCR. The reasons for setting up specialised field units for the RARP are mainly to do with the shortage of qualified staff in the Ministry of Works provincial engineers offices and, perhaps more significantly, the fact that the RARP is, in large part, financed by external funds. The Mexican programme on the other hand is almost entirely financed by government funds. Whilst the Kenya RARP is proving to be a model for application elsewhere it would be more appropriate if such programmes were implemented within the structure of the public works ministry to ensure the involvement of its personnel. This would also be in line with the general philosophy that the use of labour-based methods should not be separated into a distinct programme, as if it were something of an oddity, but integrated into the framework of the operational ministries. This comes over clearly in Nilsson's paper. He strongly recommends that one should not set up separate systems of training, management administration and procurement for labour-based programmes, but modify and adapt the existing systems to allow their effective use. Glaister points out the Rural Development Department constructs tertiary roads on a self-help basis using labour-based methods whilst the Ministry of Public Works constructs primary and secondary roads using equipment. This division is not conducive to an acceptance within the Ministry of the use of labour-based methods. In fact it tends to reinforce the natural bias against their use on any projects except those constructed under relief programmes.

In the planning of a labour-based programe one of the major problems is in assessing the level of productivity that can be achieved. McCutcheon notes how difficult this was, not only because of lack of data, but because of the wide variations in that which does exist. What is clear is that the productivity achieved on *traditional* labour-based schemes is grossly inferior to that on a well-organised, well-planned labour-based programme. Furthermore, motivation has a great deal to do with the level of productivity achieved. If the workers feel that the road they are constructing will be of direct benefit to them they are likely to achieve a reasonable level of productivity. This was clearly recognised in the Mexican programme. Moreover, whilst financial incentives do increase productivity this has to be viewed in relation to the present income and level of employment of the workers. In India and Kenya where the level of underemployment is high, the introduction of task rate working was sufficient to increase productivity. It is interesting to note that even in the self-help project on Afghanistan task work was introduced to increase productivity.

Incentives and community spirit can increase productivity. However, innovations also have a role to play. Whilst the World Bank's view[1] is that the prospects of using "intermediate technologies" to improve productivity has been much overrated it is fair to point out that this conclusion is based on limited experience. Certainly the type of innovations made in the Philippines[2] can greatly increase the competitiveness of labour-based methods. Howe and Barwell's paper shows that there is a wide range of light equipment which could be developed effectively and that, to date, the amount of effort directed towards this aspect has been minimal when compared with the resources poured into the development of heavy construction equipment.

Little work has so far been done on the measurement of benefits that accrue through the use of labour-based methods in road construction. In general the benefits are assumed: increased employment, increased rural income, development of small-scale manufacturers, better access to markets and social services. Whilst this could be the subject of a book in itself, certain aspects are worth examining here.

Employment is the most obvious, direct benefit. The great majority of the workers hired on the various programmes discussed were hired on a casual basis. This was for various reasons: ease of administration, seasonal fluctuation of supply, the dispersed nature and limited length of the projects. "Casual" has, however, various interpretations. In the Border Roads Organisation the "casual labour" may have worked with the BRO for years. In the Mexican Programme the average duration of employment was less than a month, whilst in Kenya 4-6 months is about average. Naturally, the shorter the duration the less is the benefit not only as regards income but also in terms of skill acquisition and physiological changes.

Even limited employment has substantial impact. The average increase of family income for workers on the Mexican programme was 15 per cent. Nevertheless, the ultimate object in the application of appropriate construction technology is a general increase in productive employment. It is perhaps a little unfair to criticise the programmes so far initiated for not providing more stable employment. They are isolated programmes, as yet, hopefully paving the way for a more general application. The criticism becomes somewhat cyclical. Appropriate construction technology must be adopted on a large scale in order to have an impact on employment. For this to happen demonstration projects must be set up which, by themselves, have little impact on employment.

The question of skill acquisition is perhaps more pertinent. In the long term, is one looking for underemployed workers to provide the basis of the workforce, or is one looking for the development of a construction labour force? Presumably the latter. However, this will take more time, even assuming that labour-based methods are implemented on a large scale both in the public and private sectors. What can be done now however is to ensure that there is a basis for the development of this labour force. This can be assisted by selecting from within the labour force those with management potential, for supervisor jobs. If appropriate construction technology achieves growing acceptance there will then be at least a cadre of people capable of implementing the work on the site. That some of those trained may choose to set up in business as private contractors should be viewed as a benefit not a loss. Angus Austen has shown that these people would have the means by which they could break out of the series of constraints that limit the development of the domestic construction sector.

The increase in income, particularly in the rural areas, should mean that more money is available for investment with a likely increase in agricultural production and rural industrial activities. However, there are constraints here. First the construction of the rural road will not produce development, only the means by which it can take place. The complementary activities of extension services, social and welfare facilities must also take place. In this regard the construction of rural roads must be integrated into an over-all rural development framework for the expected benefits to take place. Second, as the Mexican programme has shown, the workers are generally the poorest of the population. The increase in income therefore allows them to rise up to or above the subsistence level, but not to the state where they can accumulate savings or use the money for increasing their agricultural yield. The people who benefited most from the Mexican programme were the rural elite, a minority no doubt, who could use the extra income for purchasing more land, better fertilisers or for planting a second crop. Nevertheless, the fact that 70 per cent of the investment in the Rural Access Roads Programme remains in the rural areas does indicate that this type of programme provides an effective means for initiating rural development.

One natural by-product of the use of labour-based methods is the need for a large number of good quality hand tools and light equipment. This presents an opportunity for the small-scale manufacturer to meet this demand and develop his business.

The essays in this book indicate the depth of knowledge already accumulated on the use of labour-based methods. They also show what still needs to be done.

Angus Austen's critical analysis of the problems facing the construction industry of developing countries shows clearly that we know very little about the sector of the economy within which one is proposing a modification of resource use. As he points out, in many countries the sector is not even recognised as a separate entity. Much more work needs to be done in defining the needs and basic statistics of the industry, so that effective programmes can be initiated for its development[3].

At the other end of the scale, it is clear that the work on tools and equipment has merely scratched the surface. Not only must the existing knowledge be catalogued (as in the forthcoming ILO *Guide to Tools and Equipment for Labour-Based Road Construction*) but also money must be invested in the development of tools and equipment.

We have talked a great deal about the need for commitment; however we have also recognised that "to see is to believe". Programmes like the Kenyan RARP provide a live demonstration of the viability of labour-based techniques. It will however be necessary to initiate more of these demonstration projects if engineers and policy makers are to be convinced.

Often information on new ideas tends to circulate among those who are already convinced of their rationality. The dissemination of information on the new ideas should really have two levels. First, what might be called propaganda material to policy makers to make them aware of the basic arguments. Second, detailed information to those who wish to attempt to implement the idea. McCutcheon makes a plea for a more concerted effort to provide specific information in a form which is immediately usable.

There has been recently a recognition of the need for construction management training. As Austen points out, however, it is vital that this type of training includes in it the presentation of the wide range of technologies available and the problems associated with the implementation of labour-based as well as equipment-based technologies.

Finally, transportation is a system of road and vehicle. To date the work on appropriate technology has concentrated on the road and its construction assuming that the vehicles that travel on them are the most appropriate. There is certainly a strong case to be made for the use of simpler vehicles, particularly in the rural areas, which are more in keeping with the needs and resources of the rural population[4].

There is now sufficient evidence both in the form of data and live projects, to show that labour-based methods are technically and economically viable. Many engineers are now taking the matter seriously. There are in-built prejudices which it will take time to change. However, the facts are there for those who care to see them. For policy makers and politicians the decision is less of a technical nature than one based upon broad socio-economic considerations. The use of labour-based methods would seem, however, to meet all the criteria upon which development planning is based. They serve the mass of the population, their implementation can involve popular participation in the decision-making process, they are an instrument of self-reliance, they can enhance the potential for rural development and they can, by providing income, serve to improve the standard of living of the mass of the population. Why, one might ask, is their use not being implemented on a larger scale? The answer to that question is perhaps more political than rational. The means are available, what is now required is the will to use them.

**Notes and references**

[1] IBRD, *Substitution of Labour and Equipment in Civil Construction Phase II Report*, Washington, 1974.

[2] D. Lal, Men or Machines, ILO, Geneva, 1978.

[3] The ILO and the World Bank have recently initiated a series of studies on the construction industry in developing countries.

[4] I. Barwell and J.D.G.F. Howe, "Appropriate transport facilities for the rural sector in developing countries", ILO background paper prepared for the UNIDO World Forum on Appropriate Industrial Technology, Delhi, Nov. 1978.

36.80